Carrauntoohil & MacGillycuddy's Reeks

A Walking Guide to Ireland's Highest Mountains

Jim Ryan is a civil engineer living in Cork. A habitual mountain walker, he has climbed all over the world and has written extensively on his expeditions. His guide to Aconcagua and the Central Andes was published in 2004. Jim has a particular interest in geology and claims that his spiritual home is on the Reeks of Kerry.

W0007532

Carrauntoohil & MacGillycuddy's Reeks

A Walking Guide to Ireland's Highest Mountains

Jim Ryan

The Collins Press

Published in 2006 by
The Collins Press
West Link Park
Doughcloyne
Wilton
Cork

Ryan, Jim
    Carrauntoohil & MacGillycuddy's Reeks : a walking guide to
    Ireland's highest mountains
    1. Hiking - Ireland - Macgillycuddy's Reeks - Guidebooks
    2. Macgillycuddy's Reeks (Ireland) - Guidebooks
    I. Title
    796.5'22'094196

    ISBN-10: 1905172338
    ISBN-13: 978 - 1905172337

Typesetting and design: Stuart Coughlan at edit+

Font: Myriad Pro Light 9 point

Printed in Spain

Title page: Cummeenapeasta Ridge from Cruach Mhór

Author's and Publisher's Caution

Climbing and hillwalking are dangerous pastimes and they are fraught with many perils. In this book attempts have been made to highlight some of these perils. However, it is not possible to list all of them.

The basic assumption of the author and publisher is that those who follow the walks listed in this book are persons with the experience and capabilities commensurate with these activities.

Acknowledgements

This book has been some years in the making and I have walked these mountains with many different people, gaining a little from each of them. I thank Dr Ivor McCarthy for helping me with the geology, Brian Madden and Eugene McMorrow of Ordnance Survey Ireland for producing the maps, Timmy Doyle for his memoirs, Jim Wilson for the pictures of birds, Eileen Tangney from the Black Valley, Sheila Doona from Lough Acoose, and the Cronin family from Meallis. I was helped by Sean Ryan, who has a wealth of knowledge of the Reeks, and by Michael Carey, walk leader with the Bishopstown Hillwalkers whose experience of maps and routes is second to none. Thanks are due to those mentioned in the section People of the Reeks. This has been a labour of love for me and my neighbour Con Collins. I thank my family for their forbearance, their help and suggestions, and hours of proof reading.   ***Jim Ryan***

Carrauntoohil from the Hag's Glen in winter

Contents

The Walks

The Gap Of Dunloe Area

Safe Ascents & Descents on Carrauntoohil

Hag's Glen Eastern Side

Hag's Glen Western Side

Routes from Glencar

The Reeks Walks

The Black Valley and the Bridia Valley

Low Level Walks

Maps

USING THIS BOOK

Maps, Grid References and GPSs

The maps in this book are extracted from the Ordnance Survey Ireland (OSI) 1:25,000 map of the MacGillycuddy's Reeks. They were produced by OSI and are subject to copyright.

GPSs should be configured to the Irish Grid, with units in metres.

Throughout this book key landmarks are given using Ordnance Grid References. For example: Carrauntoohil is at grid reference Height: **1039** Longitude: **80360** Latitude: **84415.** The six-digit conventional reference would be **803844** i.e. the first three digits of the GPS co-ordinates.

The longitude refers to the horizontal distances between the vertical grid lines. Since the longitude and latitude grid lines are somewhat similar to each other in this area it is important not to mistake one for the other.

The GPS reading is only as good as the satellites it can track. In mountainous areas the surrounding high ground will often obscure satellites. In gullies, for instance, a GPS will have limited accuracy.

Above right: *Jim Ryan (standing) with friends at dawn on the summit of Beenkeragh*

Walk Times, Ascents

The common time calculation of one hour for every 400m ascent and one hour for every 4 km of flat walking should generally agree with the walk times given in this book. The ascents given are the cumulative ascents over the walk.

Escape Routes

Escape routes are suggested in case of an emergency, where it is imperative that one has to descend to lower ground. They are not intended as alternative routes.

Access to Lands

The walks shown in this book are generally over private property. Although much of the lands are classed as commonage, this merely relates to their ownership in common by a number of people. There are few rights of way, except on public roads, so that the walker enters the lands at the discretion of the owners.

The Country Code

Hillwalkers should be familiar with the country code of leaving no trace. Please do not block gateways or access points, close all gates, do not interfere with fences, ensure that sheep and other farm animals are not interfered with, make as little noise as possible, remove all rubbish, even if it is not your own.

MACGILLYCUDDY'S REEKS
A PROFILE

Ireland's Highest Mountains

The MacGillycuddy's Reeks are Ireland's highest mountains. They include the country's three highest peaks, all over 1000 m: Carrauntoohil which soars to 1039 m, nearby Beenkeragh which has a height of 1010m and Caher at 1001 m.

The Reeks stretch from the picturesque Gap of Dunloe in the east to Glencar in the west. Within this relatively confined area of 100 square km there is great natural beauty and wild rugged mountain terrain. The placenames are evocative and give some sense of the history and charm of this part of Kerry: Hag's Glen, The Big Gun, Eagle's Nest, The Devil's Ladder and the Hag's Tooth. Attracting over 25,000 walkers each year, the area is a wonderful natural resource.

As the numbers increase, the degree of tragedy on the mountains multiplies. Between 1966 and 2000 there were seventeen fatalities on the Reeks, equating to one every second year. Since 2000 this rate has increased to two per annum. Many come ill-prepared, lacking proper gear, possibly without even a map. The routes up the Reeks are not clearly marked; the mountains are covered in mist for three-quarters of

Previous page: *Cruach Bheag*

The Reeks from Maolán Buí

the time; it is therefore essential for visitors to have a basic knowledge before entering the area.

In books that describe the climbing routes on the Reeks the information provided is often scant. The main purpose of this book is to indicate with clear maps and photographs a variety of popular trails. The route descriptions give grid reference locations of important landmarks. This will enable the hillwalker to discover, either with a map and a compass or a GPS, where he/she is and what direction to take.

Climbing a mountain should never be simply about getting to the top. It is in these wild and secluded places that we see nature at its best. There is much to interest the hillwalker, from the wonder of how the mountains were formed in the first place to the creatures and plants that make them their home. A secondary purpose, therefore, is to make a visit to this part of Kerry as memorable and enjoyable as possible. Thus information is provided on the geology, history, flora and fauna of the Reeks.

GEOLOGY

The Bedrock of the Reeks

The bedrock of the Reeks is composed generally of sandstones of varying particle size, which are collectively known as the 'Old Red Sandstone'. These rocks date from the Devonian Period (410 to about 350 million years ago) when Ireland was located in a hot, arid, equatorial setting. During these 60 million years, southern Ireland was the site of a major sedimentary basin known as the Munster Basin in which sediment accumulated to an enormous thickness. Most of Counties Kerry and Cork was a vast low-lying alluvial plain into which seasonal rivers drained southwards. The layers of sediment which were deposited on the alluvial plain formed the Old Red Sandstone and were derived from a mountainous area to the north. Chemical oxidation resulted in much of the sediment becoming stained with a distinctive red or purple colour. This is due to the mineral haematite, a form of iron oxide.

The composition of the Old Red Sandstone is variable. It contains mudstones, fine to coarse grained sandstones, quartz pebbly sandstones and the concrete-like quartz conglomerates of varying colours. Outcrops of quartz conglomerate are visible at the base of the Turf Path in the Gap of Dunloe, on the Beenkeragh Ridge, at Tomies Chimneys and the northern side of Purple Mountain at Cathair and Tomies. Boulders of quartz conglomerate are dispersed throughout the Reeks at many locations.

Quartz conglomerate rock

The sedimentary layers of the Iveragh Peninsula can be subdivided into three rock formations: the Lough Acoose Formation, the Chloritic Sandstone Formation and the Ballinskelligs Sandstone Formation in ascending order. The cumulative thickness of these layers is quite startling, being in excess of 7 km.

Old Red Sandstone is not particular to the south of Ireland. It is also common in many parts of Britain. It dominates the bedrock of southwest Ireland and is easily identifiable by its distinctive red/purple colour. However, in some areas the Devonian rocks contain green bands, such as the green chloritic sandstones which outcrop extensively in the Reeks. The green colour was caused in part by chemically reducing conditions which resulted in iron minerals being changed to a green ferrous form. This occurred where sediment was deposited in an oxygen-deficient environment caused by high water tables. Elsewhere, green colours are due to the presence of the metamorphic mineral chlorite.

There are virtually no fossils in the Old Red Sandstone. Animals and plants were sparse due to the harsh climate and their preservation in the sediment would have been limited due to the vigorous oxidising conditions.

The Devonian Period was followed by the Carboniferous Period when most of the Munster Basin became submerged beneath a northerly advancing deepening sea which ultimately covered most of Ireland.

Formation of the Reeks

At the end of the Carboniferous, about 290 million years ago, the sediment layers were deformed by the Variscan phase of mountain building. This consisted of northward-directed tectonic forces similar to the present-day collision of India with Asia which is continuing to construct the Himalayan mountain chain.

The Variscan deformation resulted in the rock layers being folded and thrust up into a series of major east-west trending anticlinal and synclinal folds. In general, the anticlinal areas correspond to the peninsular areas of the southwest while the synclines occupy the bays and wide valleys. Several orders of folds are developed so that small-scale folds are superimposed on the major folds. This explains how synclines such as the Inny Syncline are located within the Iveragh Peninsula. The

Variscan deformation also resulted in a multitude of fractures in the bedrock which include faults, joints and closely spaced cleavage planes. A prominent fault is located immediately to the east of Carrauntoohil, under the Beenkeragh Ridge.

The mountains of Kerry and Cork are the denuded remnants of the original Variscan Mountain chain. Erosion during much of the past 290 million years has removed all of the Carboniferous deposits and a substantial amount of Devonian sediments which were initially laid down. Although Carrauntoohil today is 1039m high, it may have originally been over 4000 m in height.

The Ice Ages

Ireland was glaciated many times during the past 1.8 million years. Much of the landscape of the Reeks region is the product of weathering and erosion during the last two glacial stages known as the Mousterian (300,000-130,000 years ago) and Midlandian (80,000-10,000 years ago) cold stages. The major centre of ice accumulation was located to the west of Kenmare from which ice radiated outwards in all directions.

Ice moved northwestwards from Kenmare Bay through the Caragh valley to the west of the Reeks. Tongues of ice also moved northwards from Kenmare Bay through Lady's View and possibly through the Gap of Dunloe onto the Killarney plain. Evidence for this lies in the splendid development of *roches moutonneés,* of which Brassel Mountain is a good example. These are asymmetrical mound-like forms in the bedrock which developed as a result of ice movement. The steep side of these erosional structures face away from the source of the ice. Other evidence comes from the extensive development of glacial *striae*, which are scratches in the bedrock caused by boulders being dragged over them by the ice.

The ice also resulted in deposits of sediment known as moraines. These are mounds of boulders set within soil which accumulated at the margins (lateral moraines) of ice flows and at their ends (terminal moraines). A terminal moraine can be seen south of the Gap of Dunloe at Derrycarna adjacent to Drishana Mountain. The ice temporarily came to a standstill here and dropped its load of glacial sediment. A river has recently cut through the moraine leaving relatively unstable cliffs at this point.

Left: *The line of the major fault under the Beenkeragh Ridge, north of Lough Cummeenoughter*
Above: *Stump of an oak tree emerging from the bog in Hag's Glen*

Local mountain glaciers developed on the flanks of the Reeks resulting in a classic series of corries or cirques (known in the southwest of Ireland as *coom*). The highest peaks of the Reeks projected above the ice and were subjected to severe ice weathering due to freezing of water within cracks in the rock. This has resulted in the opening up of fractures in the bedrock and has given the mountain tops their jagged appearance. The topography of the Reeks contrasts with the relatively smooth forms of the Galtees and the Wicklow Mountains which were probably fully glaciated.

Bog Formation

Warm, humid conditions starting about 9000 years ago saw the formation of blanket bogs. These conditions continued until about 4500 years ago. By then a major part of County Kerry was covered by blanket bog. The formation of blanket bog changed somewhat about 4500 years ago, with a peat that was of uniformly high humus content giving way to a peat of varying humification. The stump of a pine tree, dating from about 4500 years ago, was found at a level of 250m on the Reeks.

Blanket bog is still formed today as areas with rainfall in excess of 1250mm cause water logging of the ground.

HISTORY

Neolithic Farmers

As the ice retreated and the land warmed it is doubtful there was much habitation in the area of the Reeks prior to 4000 years ago. By then there were Neolithic communities flourishing in the Killarney area, spilling out to Beaufort and the valleys north of the Reeks.

Some of the original mountain cairns were thought to have been burial sites of the late Neolithic age. At Gortboy, near where the Gaddagh River flows out of Hag's Glen, a decorated late Neolithic grave is evidence of early settlement. In the valley from Beaufort to Glencar the early Ordnance maps show numerous ring forts that may have originated in the Iron Age. The remains of souterrains can be seen to the west of Lisleibane. The three that are marked on the Ordnance map are now closed up and show only as a faint feature.

Archaeological sites dot the Ordnance map also in the Bridia Valley. An example is featured in the walk of the Lough Duff Circuit where an isolated rock under the mountain of Broaghnabinnia is decorated with ancient art in the form of a fish.

Lisleibane itself was an ancient ring fort. Today it is a circular raised enclosure, with holly and other trees forming its perimeter and with a pile of stones in the centre, possibly the remains of some structure. It can be located at Grid Reference **158:82800:87650**: The feature is north

Left to Right: *Ancient ringfort of Lisleibane seen from the air; Ogham stones at Beaufort; Parkavonear Castle at Aghadoe*

east of the Lisleibane car park.

Between 2400 and 600 BC there was intense human settlement in the Killarney area, where copper and later iron were mined. The copper mine at Ross Island in Killarney was the oldest copper mine in North Western Europe. Between the years 1804 to 1829 it exported 5000 tons of copper ore to smelters in Britain.

Ogham script was the early form of literacy from the turn of the millennium until about 500 AD In a souterrain in Coolmagort near the Gap of Dunloe seven ogham stones were recovered in 1838. Other Ogham stones were found covering souterrains in the area. On the road from Beaufort to the Gap of Dunloe, and close to the latter, there is a fine display of these Ogham stones inside a railed enclosure.

From the Middle Ages to the Present Time

The Irish clans that dominated this area of Kerry were the McCarthys, the O'Sullivans and the O'Donoghues. Where the River Loe joins the River Luane is a site of strategic importance, commanding the passage over both rivers and the pass from the mountains. Although there is thought to have been a fort here, possibly built by the O'Sullivans, the Normans are credited with building Dunloe Castle in 1207 as a fortress against the Irish. In the late thirteenth century Dunloe Castle was seized by O'Sullivan Mór.

At Aghadoe, overlooking the Killarney valley, there are the remains

Left: *The tower house of Dunloe Castle*

Right: *Father Sears and the men of the Black Valley head off for a day on the construction of the new church in 1955*

of a fine Norman fortress. Parkavonear Castle was built in the thirteenth century, and is unusual in that it is cylindrical, rather than square, in shape.

Following the Desmond rebellion of 1569-1583 the area was the scene of conflict during which the chief of the O'Donoghues was killed. When this rebellion was put down one of the surveyors of the lands, Sir Valentine Browne, acquired Dunloe Castle from Donal McCarthy. O'Donoghue Mór's lands were confiscated. An account of the confiscated lands of 1584 recorded '... there are diver's timberwoods upon these landes, but no means to make commodities of them by reason that they lie in such remote mountains ...'

Cromwellian forces led by General Ludlow descended on Kerry in 1652 and great damage was suffered by the castle and the surrounding area in these years. From the mid sixteenth century to the mid nineteenth century a mini ice age occurred and there are records that the mountains were rarely without snow.

A map dated 1756 was produced by Charles Smith. In the area of the Reeks, which he called Mac Gullycuddy's Reeks, he noted that: 'This land is entumber'd with vast mountains, bogs and rocks.' The English agriculturist, Arthur Young in 1777 noted that: 'These mountains are not capable from climate of being applied to useful purposes.'

Lough Gouragh comes from the Irish *Loch Gabhrach* which means the lake of the area abounding in sheep, and Beenkeragh is the anglicised version of *Binn Chaorach*, or the peak of sheep. There are accounts in the annals that the mountains were used for the grazing of great herds of goats between 1750 and 1800 and that sheep replaced what goats were left after the famine.

The legendary Kate Kearney lived in the Gap of Dunloe in the years before the famine. Her thatched cottage, or *sibín* (pronounced sheebeen), was infamous for the production and sale of *poitín* (pronounced poiteen), an alcoholic colourless liquid distilled from potatoes.

The famine of 1846 devastated Ireland until 1851. The recovery of the population was slow and many homesteads that had been vacated were never again inhabited. In 1850 there were reputed to be six families resident in the Hag's Glen.

In 1891 the government set up the Irish Land Registry, which provides excellent records of ownership of lands to the present day. In the early part of the twentieth century the Irish Land Commission carried out a redistribution of lands in the Reeks and the ownership of some of the lands dates to these times.

From Victorian times it became the custom for some English gentlemen to climb mountains and the Reeks received a minor degree of attention before the First World War and during the inter-war years. For the poor sheep farmers a day guiding on the Reeks was a lucrative day's work and they soon became experienced at finding their way up the mountains.

The people of The Black Valley have a long tradition of community spirit. Here families with surnames such as O'Donoghue, Casey, O'Connor, O'Sullivan, Moriarty, Falvey and Tangney have a proud lineage. This was never seen more strongly than in the early 1950s when the community, led by their priest, built the Church of Our Lady of the Valley.

*Timmy Doyle's father broke stones in the Gap of Dunloe.
This picture was taken by a passing Yank*

EVICTED FROM THE GAP OF DUNLOE

This essay was written by Timmy Doyle. It is a vivid account of his family's life in the Gap of Dunloe and the Black Valley in the early 1950s. Despite the hardship of his childhood Timmy went on to join An Gárda Siochána, the Irish police, where he rose to the rank of inspector. He is the author of two books, **Peaks and Valleys**, *from which this piece is extracted, and* **Get Up Them Steps***, which recounts his experiences in An Gárda Siochána.*

My father was the best man I knew. His people came from the foothills of the MacGillycuddy Reeks (known locally as *The MacGillycuddy's*) and it was said he hadn't been born but quarried!

He was low sized and light hipped, with a strong muscular upper body and powerful arms. He was as durable as the mountains from which he came. He had little schooling, being barely able to read and write his name. But, as he said himself 'what use was writing when his pencil was the sixteen-pound sledge?' My father had other, better ways of getting his message across. He was a man of action. He didn't tell people how to do things, he showed them.

One of my earliest memories was of my father coming home from the MacGillycuddy's with this huge sledge on his shoulder. In one motion he would twirl the weapon by the handle and fling it to one side, its heavy snout rupturing the grass margin. He watched as I grabbed the massive weapon, struggling to move it and finally collapsing on top of it. Reaching down he would grab me by one arm and then, with the other, he would expertly raise the sledge over his head. After this exhibition I would help him drag the gigantic weapon to its place in the shed.

After supper each evening my father would sit by the window and my mother would hand him an old Brylcream jar which contained salve for his calloused hands. It was a local cure made from goose grease.

My mother had a richness of words whenever she wanted them. If he had the brawn, she had the brain. She was educated and read books with the light of a candle in bed at night. Another skill which attracted a lot of admiration was her ability to write a letter from start to finish without stopping to think. She came from Firies and together my parents had put down strong roots in Dunloe. She was the boss of everything that crossed our threshold. 'I think we'll leave that to herself', was my father's verdict on anything complicated that came in the door. Whatever she said was the law.

We lived at Dunloe Lodge and I was the third eldest. I was very proud of my home. I felt that the address was notable. Also, our location commanded a fantastic view of the Gap of Dunloe. Directly outside our gate the roads from Killarney and Beaufort met, and a third, dusty, spidery road slithered away to the Gap. Consequently lots of traffic passed my door. As a small child I spent many hours looking through the bars of the gate at the continuous trek of coaches, ponies, traps and side cars laden with foreign visitors heading towards the Gap with exclamations: *Bravo! Belle! Magnifique!*

From the instant my eyes could form shapes I was enchanted by the MacGillycuddy's. They seemed to have a life of their own, cloaked in contrasting textures as the day progressed. At morning, lazily waking as dawn pulled back her misty covers, glinting shadowy and burnishing with astonishing hues at midday, and in the evening sultry or brooding in preparation for oncoming darkness.

Before I could walk I was a climber.

Before I could walk I was a climber. Born to explore the mighty peaks, I began to practice on the double gate in front of our lodge. One day my eldest brother, Danny, got fed up with me, whooshed me on top of the gate and left me hanging and screeching like a stuck pig.

Sometimes the weather was frightening. The thunder lived up amid the heather and stones. It spoke, often bellowing like a thousand mad bulls. It terrified me and I felt sure the mountains would fall on top of us. One evening when the thunder trembled my mother pulled me to her and whispered 'That's your Dada breaking a big rock.' God! I couldn't wait to be a sledge man.

Just after my fifth birthday we were banished from the Gap of Dunloe. This came about suddenly. My mother was expecting her fifth child. I sensed her withdrawal and grew bold for attention. The big double gate outside our door was like a magnet, and anytime it opened or closed I was entwined like a spider on its ornamentation. This proved to be the catalyst that heralded our homelessness. I was then too young to realise the power the lady of The Big House had over our lives; she owned everything inside the gate, including us. Apparently there were conditions attached to our lodge tenancy. One of the most binding was that the big gate should remain closed at all times except when she wanted to enter or leave. In that event one or other of my parents should be present to perform that task. From the cot I can remember the hooting of the horn and my parents rushing out to minister to the Model T and its owner.

So, at the age of five, whenever the gate opened and closed I clung to it, squawking my head off. Instead of receiving a sweet or a *lucky bag* for this entertainment, the lady of the Big House took offence and headed for the parish priest. Her complaints encompassed not only me but also our expanding family. Apparently she took exception to my mother's expectant state – again!

'When is it going to stop? Bringing all those children into the world. It's disgraceful. What hope is there for them? In the name of all that's holy, you should speak to her and put a stop to it.'

She was not pleased with Father Sear's response. 'My dear lady, those children are the most precious creatures inside that gate', he said.

That ruffled her into action. The day that my new baby brother arrived was the day my father had a letter from the Big House. He didn't have to read too well to make out the black print at the top of the page. **NOTICE TO QUIT**. 'We have a boy but no home for him', he was heard to mutter later.

So my brother's homecoming was more like a wake than a celebration. But, within a few days, a house in the Black Valley was being mentioned. For me the name conjured up images of a dark, forbidding place where the sun never shone. An image reinforced by the litany after the rosary each night: Hail, holy Queen ... mourning and weeping in this valley of tears.

I can still remember the day in early December when we heaped our belongings into the lorry trailer and set off through the Gap of Dunloe for the Black Valley. It was an adventure as far as Kate Kearney's Cottage. Then the hardship set in. The road petered away to a dirt track. Up close

Through the Gap of Dunloe

the boulders were huge, magnificent, overwhelming. I will remember until the day I die the awesome feeling when I saw the Gap open up before me. How was it possible to gouge a crucible out of the mountain? I looked at my father. Had he been part of it? As if to confirm he was, he pointed out the landmarks as we progressed: the Black Strame, Coosaun, Echo and Serpent Lakes, the Peep O'Day, Gap Cottage, Madman's Seat, Gentleman's and Toas Doyle's Rock, the Colleen Bawn, the Barracks ... 'Four and a half miles of torture, boy but the tourists love it ...'

Nature had combined with man in constructing the wonders of this rugged mountain path. On either side was a sheer drop to the lakes. Then there were sharp inclines and unbelievably acute curves in the roadway which caused us to reverse and creep forward at a snail's pace. Most forbidding of all were the towering rock faces on either side, barely necklaced together and bound to fall on us at any second.

'Don't look up we're at Turnpike,' my father jumped down and ran ahead to direct us. Ahead was a huge rock, sliced in two halves to allow the minimum space to progress. The location, plus another sheer incline and a sharp right bend, made negotiation very difficult. But the worst was to come in the shape of the shoulder of Carrauntoohil.

Looking ahead the dusty pathway snaked upwards, disappearing and reappearing by turns, the lorry began skidding and losing ground. We ended up heaving tea chests on the road to lighten the load. My mother got out and began to walk, holding Thomas in her arms. Pushing and shouting we all helped the old truck up and over the summit until we heard my father shout that we were through the Gap.

Then we rested on the flat nothingness, with the lorry snorting and stuttering behind us from her exhaustion. The driver drew a bucketful of water from a nearby waterfall and splashed it over the foaming engine. Then we moved on again, until immediately below us was the Black Valley. All my fears went away and my first feeling was joyous wonder. The spectre of darkness vanished as the valley shimmered below. It should, I thought, be rechristened the *Valley of Light*. Especially for us it seemed, a pale horseshoe of a rainbow hung like a bucket handle along its eastern flank, while away to the west the watery sun splayed out shafts of golden light.

We moved down into the valley and I searched for our new home. Suddenly we stopped outside a low-slung cabin with a thatch roof – badly in need of a transplant. I ran in the door – and went up to my knees in water!

The first night in our two-roomed home was unforgettable. First we had the feathery drops of rain clattering onto Moma's saucepans. Later we had more guests. Their arrival was heralded by a furtive scratching up in the thatch, followed by a plopping sound at the bottom of our bed. The following day their identities were revealed when my father beat the thatch with a spade and a family of mice scattered up the mountain. I was sad that it was their turn to be evicted.

The derelict house bound us together in hardship but we were at least free and beholden to nobody. The valley people took us to their hearts and ensured that my father didn't suffer a day's idleness.

I loved our new home. I loved the ruggedness, the simplicity of life, sitting by the fire and telling stories. Even the winter was kind to us and while the snow swirled up in the crags, it let us alone. Crossing the Upper Lake in Tangney's boat for mass at Derrycunnihy was a highlight all its own.

However, my parents had decided that there was no future for us in the Valley long-term, and within a year the county council had found us a home passed Dunloe – a small cottage in the mixed farmland of mid Kerry. Of course, the mountains were still there, demanding the continual raising of the eyelids. A vast panorama now extending along the skyline; west of the coxcomb of Glencar and east to where the gentle slopes of the Tomies dipped into Lough Leane.

Seathrift near the summit of Carrauntoohil

FLORA

Trees

The largest area of native forest cover in Ireland is in County Kerry, much of it centred around Killarney. The National Park in Killarney has vast areas of sessile oak, birch, hazel and alder, and many fine specimens of arbutus, Royal Oaks and mighty alders.

Few trees can exist above 600m and no deciduous trees will be found above 300m. The northern approach to the Gap of Dunloe and the entrance to the Black Valley are fine areas of woodland. Unfortunately these woodlands are under severe threat – from rhododendron. Within Killarney National Park the species *Rhododendron ponticum* has a stranglehold on the forest. It forms dense thickets that prevent tree regeneration. The plant was introduced to Ireland in the eighteenth century principally for its wealth of colour in the late spring. It soon spread and has now established itself in the Gap of Dunloe, particularly near Gap Cottage.

Windswept holly tree near Lisleibane

The particular species of holly that is native to Kerry, and is the most widespread tree in the area, has very small leaves and gnarled trunks. The female of the species carry an abundance of red berries.

Gorse

The gorse or furze of Kerry produces a wonderful splash of yellow in the spring and early summer. To the hillwaker it may be regarded as a prickly obstacle. However, it has been, and to a certain extent continues to be, an important rural resource. Sheep, goat, cattle and deer are quite partial to gorse when there is little alternative vegetation about. Many fires in farmhouses are kindled with gorse. The yellow flowers have been used to make dye, whilst the potash from burning the wood has been used in the manufacture of soap.

Ground Level Plants

In the Gap of Dunloe, at the base of Purple and Tomies Mountains, the foxglove in spring raises its head above ferns and heather. So plentiful are these stately flowers that they dominate this area.

In the wetter, boggy grasslands one may find the delicate bog orchid. These precious flowers take five to ten years to bloom, are most delicate and should not be picked.

On higher ground the heather, of which there are three species, is the commonest ground cover. Sometimes

Top: *Gorse in full bloom middle of May* Bottom: *Bog orchid*

23

referred to as *ling* it can intermingle with mosses, crowberry, heath rushes and grasses. The hoary whitlow grass is an erect herb that has small white flowers. It is a common plant on the higher ground of the Reeks.

On Carrauntoohil, Beenkeragh and Purple Mountain, in rocky areas, the wild flower known as St Patrick's Cabbage *(Saxifraga spathularis)* is abundant, hiding amongst the rocks. These plants produce long, thin, multi-stemmed flowers in the summer (see illustration on the Tomies via the Chimneys walk). It is an unusual contrast to see a plant associated with the seaside, seathrift, flourishing alongside an Artic relic, roseroot, on the top of Ireland's highest mountain.

There is a brown moss that has a silver or whitish edge. The species is *Rhacomitrium lanuginosm* and often forms a carpet under the heather. Where the cover is a thin layer of moss, the ground can be treacherously slippery in wet conditions, particularly on the descent.

Lichens are regularly seen amongst the heathers and grasses. These fungi are often a bright, light green colour. They crave light, are long-lived (possibly older than many of the trees or heathers), love the acidic nature of the ground and, of course, indicate to us that the air is clean and unpolluted.

Left: *Foxglove*
Facing page, left:
A raven, the most common bird on the Reeks
Facing page, right: *A meadow pipit*

FAUNA

Animals

The predominant animals seen on the Reeks are sheep. This is a natural grazing area for them and they have made the Reeks their home for many centuries. Beenkeragh takes its names from *binn chaorach*, peak of the sheep. *Cummeenagearagh* translates to the corrie of the sheep and this sheltered mountain recess on the northern side of the Reeks is always filled with sheep. Occasionally one may spot a mountain goat. Wild hares and rabbits are quite common, hares on the higher ground, whilst rabbits tend to frequent the lower areas. These animals have few predators. Since the last Irish wolf dates to 1700 AD the fox and the larger birds of prey are the only threat.

In the 1860s three Japanese Sika deer were introduced into Killarney area. They now flourish throughout the Killarney National Park, occasionally seen near Tomies and Purple Mountain.

Frogs proliferate in Hag's Glen. In February and March many of the puddles and ponds alongside the paths are filled with frog spawn.

Birds

The big black birds that glide over the Reeks are ravens. They are distinguishable by their deep croaking prook, prook call. Curved Gully north of Carrauntoohil is *Eisc na bhFiach*, the fissure of the raven.

On the eastern Reeks there is a better chance of seeing meadow pippets. These small brown birds are preyed on by kestrels, merlins and falcons. Wrens are abundant throughout the Reeks, often flying to high elevations.

WHO OWNS THE REEKS

There are seventeen townlands in the area we are concerned with. They vary in extent but are generally between 1000 and 1500 acres, or 400 to 600 hectares. Thus the total area is approaching 25,000 acres (10,000 hectares).The State owns only the land east of the Purple-Tomies mountain ridge. This is part of the Killarney National Park, which is 10,289 hectares of lands to the east.

One family owns approximately 2800 acres (1133 hectares) which represents approximately 11 per cent. The remainder is owned by literally hundreds of individuals and much of it is *commonage*.

Commonage is land in which more than one person has grazing and/or other rights, and includes the Irish Land Commission. Since the Land Commission may not sell their land rights, the ownership can never become *freehold*.

Hotel Europe, which is owned by the Liebherr family, holds freehold the largest area of land in the Reeks. Their holding includes: all of the high ground either side of the Gap of Dunloe, from Purple and Tomies ridgeline down to the lower ground, from Drishana to Cnoc na Tarbh down to the lower slopes; the three main lakes in the Gap of Dunloe; the four lakes in the Hag's Glen: all the townland of Curraghmore, including Curraghmore Lake; all the townland of Capparoe. The Liebherr holding was once part of the original Dunloe Castle estate.

The actual summit of Carrauntoohil, and much of Hag's Glen in the townland of Coomcallee, is owned freehold by four individuals: Donal Doona, John O'Shea, John B. Doona and James Sullivan.

The great-grandfathers of these men bought the land from the Irish Land Commission, paying the sum of eleven shillings and two pence (70 cents today) twice a year for many decades, a payment at the time that was put together with great difficulty.

The eastern side of Hag's Glen up to Knocknapeasta and Cruach Bheag in the townland of Meallis is owned freehold by six individuals, of which Martin O'Shea and Bridget O'Shea own half. They acquired it from Daniel O'Shea, who acquired it from Patrick Curran Junior. It was originally part of the estate of Sir R. Blennerhasset.

The owners of Carrauntoohil, left to right: Donal Doona, John O'Shea, John B. Doona and James Sullivan

To the south around Lough Callee, from Knocknapeasta down to the Black Valley, the land is commonage, with 144 individuals having rights. Similarly the townland of Breanlee, from Lough Eagher up to Beenkeragh and Skregmore is commonage but only four persons here have land rights. Beenkeragh is in the townland of Coolroe and all of this townland is commonage. The land over which the concrete road, or *Hydro Road*, is situated is owned by Michael O'Sullivan, who also is a part owner of lands in the area of Cummeenagearagh. The company which operates the hydro scheme have only a wayleave over the land.

From Lisleibane in to the Hag's Teeth (small) the land is owned freehold by five people, with the owners of Carrauntoohil having a right of way in from Lisleibane.

PEOPLE OF THE REEKS

In the Gap of Dunloe some say there has always been a Kate Kearney. She was regarded as the matriarch of the area and there are tales about visitors awaiting the return of Kate from the hills.

The original, or perhaps most infamous, Kate Kearney was believed to have owned a cottage near where the current Kate Kearney's Cottage

Left: *Mary Coffey, proprietor of Kate Kearney's Cottage*
Right: *The Doona family of Lough Acoose*

is located. She made and sold *poitín*. Mary Coffey, the manageress of Kate Kearney's Cottage, although she hails from Donegal, has fitted in well in the Gap, and she is commonly regarded as the modern *Kate Kearney*.

Sheila Doona's father was a Coffey and her family has lived in the area for generations. She married a local man and the family now operate a guesthouse and camping site at Lough Acoose.

Gerry Christie is the current leader of Kerry Mountain Rescue. A medical scientist living in Tralee, Gerry advocates the enlargement of Killarney National Park to include the Reeks. The seizure of every opportunity to promote mountain safety is the goal of Kerry Mountain Rescue and Gerry is foremost in this regard.

Pat Falvey hails from Cork but now lives under Strickeen Hill. Amongst

Left to right: *Gerry Christie, leader of Kerry Mountain Rescue; Pat Falvey, mountaineer; Con Moriarty, mountaineer and authority on the Reeks*

The Cronin's of Cronin's Yard: Eileen, her son John and husband Joe

his many accomplishments he can boast summiting Everest on two occasions. Pat's *Mountain Lodge* is renowned as a source for mountain skills training, weekend retreats and activities organisation.

Con Moriarty was born and spent his childhood in the Gap of Dunloe. An accomplished climber, he joined Kerry Mountain Rescue at the age of only eighteen. Con is a Reeks walk leader and he is often called by the locals when sheep require rescuing. Con is the proprietor of a shop in Killarney that specialises in gear for hillwalkers and mountaineers. He is an authority on the placenames of the Reeks and is passionate about the retention and use of these names.

Cronin's Yard is synonymous with Carrauntoohil. Eileen Cronin lives there. Her son, John, is a member of Kerry Mountain Rescue and he has constructed well-needed facilities for hillwalkers.

This picture taken in the 1980s includes the Cronins, Con Moriarty and members of Kerry Mountain Rescue

CLIMATE

The Iveragh Peninsula in which the Reeks are situated is the wettest area of Ireland. Whereas the southeast of the country experiences only 120 rain days per annum, and the cities of Dublin and Cork suffer 150 rain days, the Iveragh Peninsula has over 200 rain days and the Reeks over 225 rain days annually.

Rainfall in the Killarney lowlands is generally 1250mm annually. The worst recorded rainfall was in 1964 when the area experienced 4265mm of rain. November is generally the wettest month. On 8 November 1941 210mm of rain was recorded at Muckross in Kerry over a 24-hour period. Above the 2000m contour the average annual rainfall increases to over 2000mm, and on the Reeks summits this figure rises to over 3000mm annually.

The Reeks are shrouded in cloud for over 75 per cent of the time and it is a rarity therefore to summit with a clear blue sky. July, oddly enough, is the cloudiest month of the year, though not necessarily the wettest. Moist, humid air from the Atlantic, carried by winds from the south and south-west, rises as it encounters the high mountains and the air condenses to form the clouds. These cumulus clouds produce mist and occasional showers but rarely heavy rain.

March, April and May have the least cloud and May is the sunniest month. December is the dullest month, with an average of only one hour's sunshine per day. February is the coldest month, whilst August is the warmest.

The temperature on the mountains drops by 1°C for every 100 to 150 m in elevation, so that, when it is 10°C in Killarney expect it to be under 3°C on the summits of the Reeks.

Left: *Horizontal icicles formed by the wind on the summit of Carrauntoohil*
Right: *Icy conditions near Heavenly Gates*

The Reeks are no different to other mountains where wind can be a major factor in terms of safety. Remarkably, Kerry has a relatively low number of gale days per annum. The meteorological station at Caherciveen in Kerry records an average of twelve gale days per year, contrasting with Malin Head which records an average of 42 gale days per annum.

January is the windiest month of the year, with average wind speeds at low level of 25 km per hour. The wind speed can be dramatically higher on the mountains, however. Hag's Glen is notorious as a bleak area on a windy day, when the winds whip down over the col of the Devil's Ladder to drive down through the valley.

Carrauntoohil from Beenkeragh on a frosty morning. The gullies of Curved, Central and O'Shea's filled with snow above a frozen Lough Cummeenoughter

PLACENAMES AND TOWNLANDS

Local Dialects

There are a few idiosyncrasies in the Reeks area that may be useful when talking to local people.

The road from the Gap of Dunloe over to Glencar is known as *The Board of Works' Road*. Lisleibane is pronounced *Lislebawn*, Carrauntoohil is *Corrawntoohil*, Fossa should sound more like *Fusa*, and the river through Hag's Glen, the Gaddagh, is pronounced *Gaddock*. Although the Ordnance map shows it as Stumpeenadaff, this is not understood in the Reeks, and Stumpa an tSáimh is pronounced *Stumpa an Tawve*. If O'Shea's gully is referred as *Brother O'Shea's Gully*, with a deep roll on the last word, chances are you are speaking to a local.

If a sheep falls off the mountain it is said that it was *clifted*.

When the Ordnance surveyors descended on the remote regions of Ireland in the 1840s an Anglicised version in the maps of the Irish placenames was often the eventual outcome.

There are a few common words that crop up regularly:

Coom, as in Coomloughra is from the Irish *com*, meaning a mountain recess, or corrie.

Cummeen comes from the Irish *coimín* which means common, as in common land or pasturage. The word is also used to refer to a valley area, as in Cummeenduff – The Black Valley. However, there are many instances where it is clear that the cummeen being referred to is in fact a small com, or small mountain recess. Examples of this are Cummeenapeasta, Cummeenoughter and Cummeenagearagh.

Cailleach was an old woman, witch or hag. Thus, *Lough Callee* translates to *Loch Caillí*, or the lake of the hag.

Eisc is a fissure, or gully in the mountain.

Breandán Ó Cíobháin, in his book *Toponomia Hiberniae - Barony of Dunkerron North*, provides much research into the possible origin of the placenames. He suggests that the sheep farmers, in their dependence on the forbidding landscape, conferred on it, by means of placenames, a personality which reflects the way of life and attitudes of the community.

Carrauntoohil with the Hag's Tooth in the foreground

The placenames contain references to poverty and squalor. For instance, Lisleibane is possibly derived from *Lios Leadhbán*, the fort of the man of tatters. Breanlee may be from *brean líghe*, a stinking stream. The Bridia Valley may come from *braighde*, a prison.

The references to hags and serpents abound but there are also many instances of places called after peculiar people – *Madman's Seat*, *False Man's Ridge (Feabrahy)*, *Gentleman's Rock*. The influence of sheep on the lives of the community is well reflected in names such as *Binn Chaorach* and *Coimín na gCaorach* but there are also a few suggestions that horses were used. The summit of Curraghmore is known as *Graighin*, which may come from *groidhin*, a place where horses are fed. There is a gully that comes from Coomloughra up to the Caher ridge which is called *The Black Mare*.

It should be noted that the last three letters of the highest peak, **Carrauntoohil**, has nothing to do with hills but is in fact derived from the Irish *corrán tuathail*, meaning inverted sickle. This was intended to describe the shape of the mountain.

Dunloe comes from the Irish *dún* or castle, and *ló*, the name of the river that flows through the Gap. However, the original name for the Gap of Dunloe, *Bearna an Choimín*, contained no reference to the castle or the river.

In 2003 the Ordnance Survey set up a consultancy scheme, when they canvassed the views of locals, hillwalkers and mountaineers on how the future map of the Reeks should look. The consensus was that the map would be too cluttered with both Irish and English placenames, and in producing the 1:25,000 map, the decision was to show only the Irish placenames.

The following is a non-exhaustive list of the more common placenames in the Reeks. It should be noted that folklorists differ on these placenames, the precise area or feature referred to and their translation or meaning.

English	Irish	Meaning
Lough Acoose	*Loch Dhá Chuais*	The lake of two caves
Lough Auger	*Loch a Tarathair*	Possibly because an auger was found there, possibly the stony bedded lake
Bearna an tSáraithe	*Bearna an tSáraithe*	Gap of the surmounting
Beenkeragh	*Binn Chaorach*	Peak of the sheep
Beaufort	*Lios an Phúca*	The fort of the fairy
Bohernagigeach	*Bóthar na Gíge*	The road (over the) pap[1]
Breanlee	*Bréinlí*	Possibly from Brean Líghe, a stinking stream
Bridia	*Braighde*	Prison
Broaghnabinnia	*Bruach na Binne*	Verge of the peak
Bunbinnia	*Bun Binne*	Bottom of peak
Capparoe	*Ceapaigh Rua*	Red plot
Carrauntoohil	*Corrán tuathail*	Inverted sickle
Caher	*Cathair*	Circular stone fort
Cappeenthlarig	*Ceapach an Chláraigh*	Plot of level ground
Cathair na Féinne	*Cathair na Féinne*	Circular stone fort of the Fianna[2]
Chimneys	*Céim an Fhia*	The jump of the deer

English	Irish	Meaning
Cillin	*Cillín*	Little burial ground – a burial ground for unbaptised babies
Cloghernoosh	*Clochar Núis*	Rock of the beestings (a type of mi
Cnoc an Bhráca	*Cnoc an Bhráca*	Hill of the hovel or rough ground
Cnoc an Chuillinn	*Cnoc an Chuillinn*	Hill of the rolling incline (or hill of the holly)
Cnoc na Tarbh	*Cnoc na Tarbh*	Hill of the bulls
Cnoc Toinne	*Cnoc Toinne*	Wave hill
Coomloughra	*Com Luachra*	The glen of the rushes
Crossderry	*Crosdoire*	Oakwood cross
Cruach Mhór	*Cruach Mhór*	Big reek or stack
Cummeenagearagh	*Coimín na gCaorach*	Mountain recess of the sheep
Cummeenduff	*Coimín Dubh*	Black common land or valley
Cummeenapeasta	*Coimín na Péiste*	Mountain recess of the serpent
Curraghmore	*Currach Mór*	Big marsh
Curved Gully	*Eisc na bhFiach*	Fissure, gully of the ravens
Derrycarna	*Doire Chárna*	Mounded oakwood
Derrynafeana	*Doire na Féinne*	Oakwood of the Fianna[2]
Drishana	*Driseán*	Little bramble
Dromluska	*Drom Loiscithe*	Burnt ridge or ridge of rushes
Eagle's Nest	*Nead an Fhiolair*	Nest of the eagle
Eisc an Bhráca	*Eisc an Bhráca*	Fissure/gully of the rough ground
Feabrahy	*Fear Bréige*	False man
Fossa	*Fossa*	Believed to come from *fosadh*, a level place.
Gaddagh	*An gheadach*	Cow with a star on her forehead
Gap of Dunloe	*Bearna an Choimín*	The gap of the commonage
Gearhameen	*Gaortha Mhín*	Smooth river valley
Killarney	*Cill Áirne*	The church of the sloes
Knockbrinnea	*Cnoc Broinne*	Hill (in the shape) of the breast
Knocknapeasta	*Cnoc na Péiste*	Hill of the serpent

English	Irish	Meaning
Lack Road	*Bóthair na Lice* (pronounced lickay)	Road of the flagstones
Lisleibane	*Lios leadhbán*	Ring fort of a tattered person
Lough Acoose	*Loch an Chuais*	Lake of the recess or bay
Lough Duff	*Dúloch*	Black Lake
Lough Gouragh	*Loch Gabhrach*	Lake where goats abound
Lough Eighter	*Lochíochtair*	Lower lake
Lyreboy	*Ladhar Bhuí*	Yellow lair
Lúib an Bhóthair	*Lúib an Bhóthair*	The bend in the road
MacGillycuddy Reeks	*Na Cruacha Dubha*	The black stacks/reeks. In English the Reeks of the son/servant of Cuddy
Maolán Buí	*Maolán Buí*	Yellow, flat hill
Meallis	*Maol lios*	Flat ring fort
Purple Mountain	*An Sliabh Corcra*	The purple mountain
Shehy Mountain	*Cnoc Seithe*	The hill of the (animal's) hide
Skregmore	*Screag Mhór*	Big rough hill
Strickeen	*Struicín*	Little peak (or possibly top of the bog)
Stuaic Bharr na hAbhann	*Stuaic Bharr na hAbhann*	The peak of the top of the river
Stumpeenadaff	*Stumpa an tSaimh*	The stump of the sorrel (a herb with a sour taste)
Tomies	*Na Toimí*	The burial ground (but possibly called after a person named Toimí)
The Turf Path	*Bóthar Chorcach*	The turf path

[1] Opinions differ on Bohernagigeach. Some suggest that it refers to the shape of the mountain here, where is resembles a woman's breast, or pap, which in Irish is *cíoch*, and of the pap would be *na cíche*. The alternative is that the area is windy, when the appropriate Irish word would be *gaoth*, so that the path's name would translate as the windy road, with of the wind becoming *na gaoithe*.

[2] Na Fianna may refer to an ancient band of warriors, known as the Fianna but it may also refer to deer in the plural.

The following are the seventeen townlands that form the area of the Reeks, from east to west, north to south:

Dunloe Lower, Dunloe Upper, Gearhameen, Coolcummisk, Alohart, Derrycarna, Cloghernoosh, Lisleibane, Meallis and Coomcallee, Capparoe, Curraghmore, Coolroe, Breanlee and Lyreboy, Coumreagh and Bunbinnia, Derrynafeana.

Cronin's Yard is in Meallis. Cloghernoosh is in the Black Valley near Brassel Mountain. Hag's Glen is in Coomcallee. The area of Glencar where the Hydro (concrete) road is located is in Breanlee.

KERRY MOUNTAIN RESCUE

The Kerry Mountain Rescue is a voluntary group of mountaineers who assist in rescuing climbers or walkers in County Kerry. Their website is **www.kerrymountainrescue.ie** and it contains advice on mountain safety and a log of all the call outs and tragedies on the Reeks since 1966.

Their headquarters is in Killarney and can be contacted any time day or night via the gardaí, by dialling 999.

Below Heavenly Gates, at map reference **587:80822:84660**, there is a mountain refuge that is maintained by the mountaineering community in Kerry. The refuge has bunk beds, blankets, fresh water and food.

ACTION PLAN FOR THE REEKS

The MacGillycuddy Reeks is an area of outstanding natural beauty and is Ireland's prime hillwalking and climbing recreation area. Its obvious future is as a national park. The national park status would safeguard the land as an area with free access to all.

Facilities for hillwalkers are sparse: car parking at Lisleibane and Glencar is inadequate; there is no public toilet except in the Gap of Dunloe which is too far away and the facilities at Cronin's Yard need to be repeated at Lisleibane and Glencar.

In 2005 Beaufort Community Council took the initiative of formulating an action plan for the Reeks. The plan envisaged a range of works to improve visitor access and walker's safety. Amongst the range of works proposed were:

- construction of a building to accommodate toilets, showers and rest areas at Lisleibane;
- construction of a surfaced car park at Lisleibane to take 36 cars;
- the erection of crossings over the Gaddagh River in the Hag's Glen;
- footpath repair and erosion control on the Devil's Ladder.

Unfortunately the plan did not meet the approval of Kerry County Council, but may be activated in the future.

GETTING THERE

Maps

The most appropriate map of The Reeks is the weatherproof 1:25,000 entitled *MacGillycuddy's Reeks*, published by the Ordnance Survey. All the placenames are in Irish.

The alternative is the Ordnance Survey's 1:50,000 number 78, which shows less placenames which are in both Irish and English.

For those who frequent the Kerry mountains on a regular basis there is the Ordnance Survey's *Trailmaster*. This is a compact disk that can be purchased from the Ordnance Survey. It contains all the maps of Kerry and parts of west Cork. The software allows the user to interface with a GPS, to plot a route, and there is a three-dimensional feature that allows the hillwalker to view the route and to fly over it.

Also available is the superwalker map, published in 2006 by Harveys, of the MacGillycuddy's Reeks. At a scale of 1:30,000 it features detail of the summit of Carrauntoohil at 1:15,000.

Killarney to the Gap of Dunloe

Killarney is a complex town; there are one-way streets and routes out of the town are not very well signposted. If you are coming in from Cork it is better to avoid the town. At the first roundabout proceed straight, rather than going left, and continue straight at the next roundabout to take you directly to the Killorglin Road.

From Killarney take the N72 towards Killorglin. Passing through the district of Fossa, after 6 km take the road that is signposted to the left to Glencar. This is a narrow, twisting road. After a further 3 km there is a sign on the left to the Gap of Dunloe. Continue into the Gap, and after a kilometre and a half there is a spacious public car park at Kate Kearney's Cottage.

From this car park one can walk up Purple Mountain or onto the Eastern Reeks. There is a public toilet and a public telephone. Kate Kearney's public house is a busy establishment, popular with locals and hillwalkers alike. Across the road is a small café.

Map 1 - West Munster

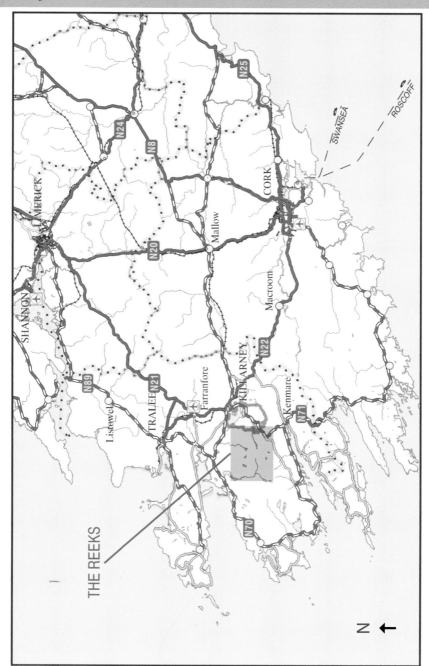

41

The Gap of Dunloe and the Black Valley

There are few places to park in the Gap of Dunloe and the Black Valley. During the summer the Gap of Dunloe is busy with jaunting cars: driving into the Gap and parking there is frowned upon by the locals. The jarvies who operate the jaunting cars through the Gap of Dunloe will not be too responsive to giving way to cars. If you do decide to drive into the Gap restrict your time there to early in the morning and late in the evening.

At the Head of the Gap there is room for a few cars. At Lúib an Bhóthair, the first hairpin into the Black Valley after the Head of the Gap, there are two parking spaces. Below Brassel Mountain there are also isolated parking areas.

Cronin's Yard

Beyond the turn to the Gap of Dunloe, and heading towards Glencar,

Cronin's Yard

after 4 km there is a crossroads with a shop and a petrol filling station: this is known as Kissane's Cross. Immediately past this crossroads there is another crossroads with a sign to the left, *Carrauntoohil 5*. This narrow road leads to Cronin's Yard.

There is a small charge to park at Cronin's. On site there are changing rooms, toilets, a public telephone and a small place to purchase snacks.

Cronin's Yard is a popular parking area for those climbing Carrauntoohil. On Sundays in particular it can be very crowded.

Lisleibane

1½ km beyond the turn for Cronin's Yard, en route to Glencar, there is a turn to the left immediately after a narrow bridge over the River Gaddagh. This unsigned road leads to the second popular parking place for Carrauntoohil. The road to Lisleibane is 2 km of poor quality that deteriorates to dirt track with potholes, and the car park is rough. There is no shelter here. Often the car park is full, when it may be necessary to park a kilometre back at the first road junction.

Lisleibane has the advantage that the route to Carrauntoohil through Hag's Glen is slightly shorter than from Cronin's Yard and does not involve a river crossing.

Glencar

From Kissane's Cross around to Lough Acoose is 11 km. It is a further 6 km from Lough Acoose to The Climbers Inn at Glencar. Apart from Lough Acoose and Glencar there are precious few places to park. The Concrete Road (or as it is noted on the map, the Hydro Road) is a good route to Lough Coomloughra but its starting point on the public road is remote from a safe parking place. A quarter of a kilometre back towards the Gap of Dunloe there is a small disused quarry that affords a few precious places, and there is a lay-by on the left-hand side of the road halfway between the Concrete Road and Lough Acoose.

At Lough Acoose there are a few areas to park on the minor road by the lake. If you drive in around Lough Acoose, through the gate and on up to Derrynafeana, there are a few parking spaces.

PRACTICALITIES

Available free at the tourist office and in most hotels and hostels is a monthly guide to Killarney. This is an excellent publication that contains a wealth of information, listing hotels, guesthouses, restaurants, places of interest, walks and events. It subdivides places to eat into cost categories, and provides telephone numbers for doctors, opticians, pharmacists, taxis, police and hospitals.

Checking the Weather Forecast

The Irish Meteorological Service, Met Eireann, has a website which gives weather forecasts **www.met.ie**. The Service also has a direct phone dial **1550 123 850** which will give the weather forecast for Munster.

www.ukie.accuweather.com is an excellent website for an accurate prediction of the weather. Simply search for the weather in Killarney to get the information.

Camping

There are two campsites in Fossa, another at Kissane's Cross and a further campsite at Glencar. The four campsites are relatively small and compact

Sunset on the Eastern Reeks from Lough Cummeenoughter

and, during the summer, should be booked in advance. The campsite at Glencar, just before Lough Acoose, is run by the Doona family, who combine camping with a house to rent and bed and breakfast. The Doonas are part owners of Carrauntoohil.

Above Lisleibane there are flat, dry areas to camp. Within Hag's Glen camping around the two main lakes is popular. Along the banks of the Gaddagh River that flows through the glen there are sheltered, flat areas where it is possible to camp.

There are few suitable tent sites high on the mountains, particularly on the western side. Any flat, sheltered areas have been colonised already by the dreaded midge, a tiny flying nuisance that bites.

The ridge of the Eastern Reeks, from Knocknapeasta to the Devil's Ladder, is soft and flat in places, though quite exposed. Bivying inside the rock enclosures on the summit of Carrauntoohil is popular, though uncomfortable.

In the townland of Capparoe, between Brassel Mountain and Cnoc an Chuillin on the Eastern Reeks, there is an ideal camping place at **750:82830:83050**. The flat grassy area is sheltered and faces south. There is a good parking place below in Dromluska, near a sheep pen at **152:82125:81925**.

Map 2 - Killarney Area

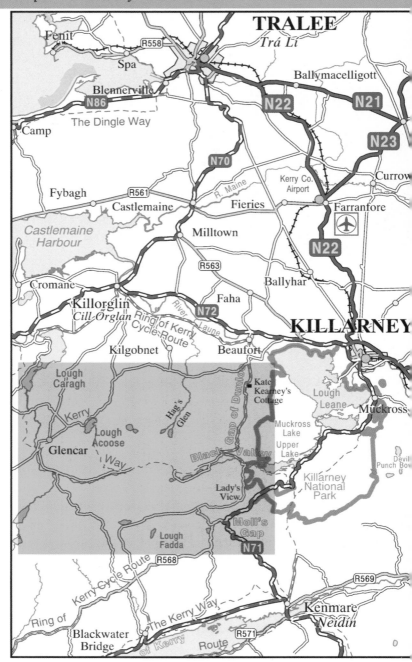

Hostels

An Óige, the Irish Youth Hostelling Association, operates two hostels near the area. These hostels are not restricted to any age group, are clean, well managed and inexpensive. They cater for individuals sleeping in dormitory accommodation or families/groups in family rooms. Kitchens are available to cook one's meal, or there is the option of being served meals.

The largest of these hostels is in Fossa, on the road to Milltown, a few hundred metres from Fossa on the left. It is a fine house in quiet grounds, with ample parking. The second hostel is in the Black Valley beside the Black Valley Church.

There is a third private hostel, the Mountain View Hostel, on the road that goes north from Kissane's crossroads.

There are a few private hostels in Killarney, and The Climbers Inn in Glencar is an inexpensive and lively hostel.

Killarney

Killarney has numerous hotels and guesthouses of all grades. This is a bustling town, with many fine restaurants, public houses, chippers and takeaways.

Because it is a tourist town it has many hotels, from five-star ratings down to hostels, with correspondingly varying prices. In the height of the Irish summer it can nevertheless be quite difficult to obtain accommodation.

Fossa

Fossa is a haven for golfers. The village is spread along the busy Killarney to Killorglin road and many of the guesthouses suffer from road noise (though not the hotels and the youth hostel). Worth a visit is the tiny church, the *Prince of Peace*, designed by one of Ireland's foremost architects Liam McCormick from Derry.

There are a number of guesthouses and some hotels at Fossa. Top of the pile for luxury and cost is the Hotel Europe (the owners of which also own much of the Reeks). Above Fossa, off the road to Milltown, is the prestigious Aghadoe House Hotel, boasting one of the finest restaurants in Ireland. Along the main road there are two restaurants and a pub.

Beaufort

Fishing is to Beaufort what golfing is to Fossa. This village is off the main road and is a very pleasant place to stay, have a meal or a drink. The people are friendly and strangers get a warm welcome.

There are two good bar-restaurants that will vie for your custom, and a collection of quiet guesthouses.

The Gap of Dunloe

Near the entry to the Gap is the Hotel Dunloe Castle, owned by the same group as the Hotel Europe. This is a spacious, luxury hotel, open only during the summer.

In the Gap there are few guesthouses, no hostels or campsites. Kate Kearney's Cottage is a lively pub and restaurant, open all year. Its clientele divides roughly equally into walkers and locals. Across the road there is a coffee shop.

Beyond the entry to the Gap, the first dirt-track road to the left leads to Pat Falvey's Mountain Lodge. This is a guesthouse run by an accomplished mountaineer, who is a professional guide, not only on the Reeks but on international expeditions. Pat runs activity weekends that includes mountain skills.

Kate Kearneys is a popular hostelry in the Gap of Dunloe

Pat Falvey's Mountain Lodge   *The Black Valley Hostel*

The Black Valley

In the Black Valley there is a youth hostel and two guesthouses. The youth hostel is allied to Hostelling International. To access these establishments requires driving through the Gap and you will have noted that, during the summer, the Gap is very busy with jaunting cars, the drivers of which frown on cars during their prime hiring times. Do, therefore, get to your guesthouse as late in the evening or as early in the morning as possible. Alternatively, take the long route out of the Black Valley to the east, then south, which will take you to Killarney via Moll's Gap.

The guesthouses in the Black Valley have the advantage that they are in an area of outstanding natural beauty, and the disadvantage, perhaps, that they are a long way from a pub.

Glencar

From the Gap of Dunloe over to Glencar there are a limited number of guesthouses. There are none on the minor roads in to Cronin's Yard or in to Lisleibane.

The Climbers' Inn is the focal point of Glencar, both for locals and walkers alike. This busy public house has its walls adorned with mountaineering memorabilia. It has hostel accommodation. There is also a hotel, a campsite and a few guesthouses in Glencar.

Map 3 - The Reeks

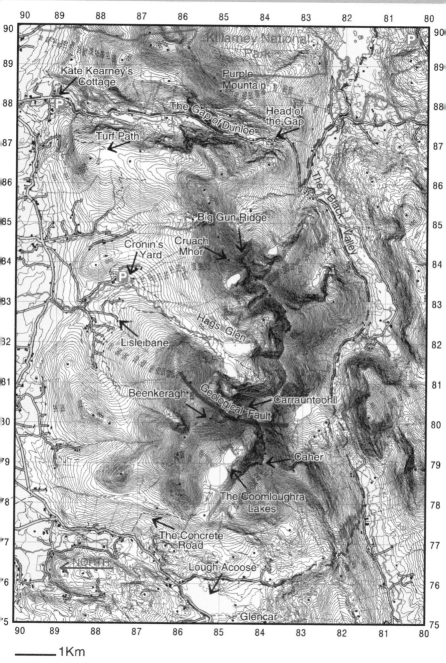

Kate Kearney's Cottage
P
Turf Path
Purple Mountain
Killarney National Park
The Gap of Dunloe
Head of the Gap
The Black Valley
Big Gun Ridge
Cruach Mhor
Cronin's Yard
P
Hags Glen
Lisleibane
Beenkeragh
Geological Fault
Carrauntoohil
Caher
The Coomloughra Lakes
The Concrete Road
NORTH
Lough Acoose
Glencar
1Km

51

The table below sets out the various walks and their relative difficulties. The difficulty rating varies from 1 to 5, with the lower numbers being easy walks and the higher numbers covering more challenging climbs.

For Rating 1 there will be no scrambling, a walk on gentle slopes. For Rating 3 and

	TITLE	COMMENTS		RATING
1	Eastern Reeks	Relatively short and gentle		
	Time: 4½ to 5 hours	Distance: 11 km	Ascent: 750m	Rating: 2
2	Purple Mountain	Long walk, virtually no scrambling		
	Time: 5 to 6 hours	Distance: 14 km	Ascent: 900 m	Rating: 3
3	Tomies via Chimneys	Steep ascent through the Chimneys		
	Time: 3 to 4 hours	Distance: 3 km	Ascent: 500 m	Rating: 4
4	Lough Googh	Precarious around Knocknapeasta, and steep descent		
	Time: 3 to 6 hours	Distance: 8 km	Ascent: 850 m	Rating: 4
5	Cummeennapeasta	Steep around Knocknapeasta		
	Time: 4 hours	Distance: 9 km	Ascent: 840 m	Rating: 4
6	Devil's Ladder	Scrambling on the Ladder		
	Time: 5 hours	Distance: 13 km	Ascent: 900 m	Rating: 4
7	Zig-zags	Safe ascent, some scrambling down the Bone		
	Time: 3½ to 4½ hours	Distance: 14 km	Ascent: 930 m	Rating: 3
8	O'Shea's Gully	A number of easy scrambles		
	Time: 5 to 6 hours	Distance: 14.5 km	Ascent: 900 m	Rating: 4
9	Curved Gully	Difficult scrambling in the gully		
	Time: 4½ to 5½ hours	Distance: 14 km	Ascent: 900 m	Rating: 5
10	Stumpa an tSiamh	Some precarious scrambling		
	Time: 5 hours	Distance: 11 km	Ascent: 870 m	Rating: 5

above there may be a degree of scrambling, and as we approach Rating 5 there will be some high steps or long, strenuous ascents with scrambling. None of the walks require the use of ropes or climbing gear.

TITLE	COMMENTS		RATING
11 Cummeenagearagh	Ascent only, difficult scrambling in the gully		
Time: 2½ to 3 hours	Distance: 4 km	Ascent: 950 m	Rating: 5
12 Coomloughra	Long arduous walk with some easy scrambling		
Time: 6 to 7 hours	Distance: 12 km	Ascent: 1200 m	Rating: 5
13 Black Mare	Ascent only, steep up to the Caher Ridge		
Time: 2 to 3 hours	Distance: 5.5 km	Ascent: 900 m	Rating: 4
14 Reeks Walk	Longest walk of the set, various scrambles		
Time: 7 to 9 hours	Distance: 18 km	Ascent: 1850 m	Rating: 5
15 Hag's Glen Circuit	Scrambling at the Big Gun and Beenkeragh Ridge		
Time: 6½ to 7½ hours	Distance: 16 km	Ascent: 1500 m	Rating: 5
16 Carrauntoohil from Black Valley	Steep descent		
Time: 5 to 6 hours	Distance: 11 km	Ascent: 1150 m	Rating: 3
17 Caher from Lack Road	Easy ascent and descent		
Time: 4½ to 5½ hours	Distance: 8 km	Ascent: 950 m	Rating: 2
18 Lough Duff	Long walk with steep ascent		
Time: 5 to 6 hours	Distance: 15 km	Ascent: 780 m	Rating: 4
19 Derrycunnihy	Virtually flat walk		
Time: 5 hours	Distance: 16 km	Ascent: 180 m	Rating: 1
20 The Kerry Way	Gentle slope up the Lack Road		
Time: 6 hours	Distance: 18 km	Ascent: 530 m	Rating: 1

The Gap of Dunloe Area

Walk 1

THE GAP OF DUNLOE AND THE EASTERN REEKS

Summary: A walk through the picturesque Gap of Dunloe, then a steep ascent over rocky ground, with occasional scrambling, up to Cnoc an Bhráca, to walk over a boggy plateau. Pause where turf was won from the blanket bog and descend via the Turf Path down to Kate Kearney's Cottage.

Time: 4½ to 5 hours   **Distance:** 11 km   **Ascent:** 750m

Start and Finish: Kate Kearney's Cottage

Escape Routes: This is not a walk with good escape routes. It is possible to descend into the Gap of Dunloe about halfway along the walk. However, the descent is very steep and the river below in the Gap is very deep. Frowning Man Rock referred to below provides a safe place on the southern part to descend.

Route Description see **map 4**

Starting at Kate Kearney's Cottage, walk along the tarmac road through the Gap of Dunloe, passing the three main lakes on the right and the minor lake on the left. The Gap of Dunloe is one of Ireland's famed beauty spots, drawing many thousands of tourists each month to walk or take a jaunting car through it. Do take the time therefore to pause and look around; wild holly flourishes here; the woodland supports a variety of wildlife and is a habitat for the cuckoo.

Choices of Ascent: Immediately before Gap Cottage (**194:87100:84360**) there is an ascent over grass and rock up between two streams. The alternative is to continue to the Head of the Gap (**207:87110:83900**) and step over the road fence. The former misses out the Drishana hilltop.

The climb from Gap Cottage is relatively direct up between the two streams. At the top there is a distinct boulder that has the appearance of a man's frowning head. It is at **536:86265:84587**.

At the Head of the Gap, and without losing elevation, turn to the west

Map 4 - The Gap of Dunloe and the Eastern Reeks

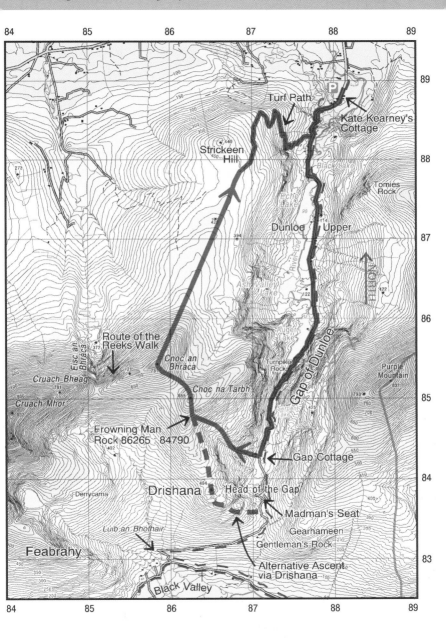

Turf Path

P

Kate Kearney's
Cottage

Strickeen
Hill

Black Lake

Tomies
Rock

Echo
Lake

Dunloe Upper

River Loe

Ash Valley
Lake

NORTH

Route of the
Reeks Walk

Cnoc an
Bhráca

Eisc an
Bhráca

Cruach Bheag

Cnoc na Tarbh

Turnpike
Rock

Gap of Dunloe

Purple
Mountain

Cruach Mhor

Frowning Man
Rock 86265 84790

Gap Cottage

Drishana

Head of the Gap

Derrycarna

Madman's Seat

Gearhameen

Luib an Bhothair

Gentleman's Rock

Feabrahy

Alternative Ascent
via Drishana

Black Valley

1Km

Turnpike Rock

and climb up over the ledges of rock to Drishana. There is no defined route. This is a climb that requires you to judge your path, possibly retracing your steps. The tendency is to climb around to the west, using grassy gullies to ascend. There are many false summits. In poor weather it is easy to bypass Drishana but do not be concerned; the ultimate goal is Cnoc na Tarbh at 655m.

Cnoc na Tarbh (hill of the bulls) has a number of enormous boulders near its summit that begs the question of how they were formed.

The next goal is Cnoc an Bhráca (hill of the hovel or rough ground) which is to the northwest, at **731:85840:85440**. There is, again, no defined path from Cnoc na Tarbh to Cnoc an Bhráca. The latter is marked by a well-constructed two-metre high cairn. Cnoc an Bhráca is part of the Reeks Walk, and so has a well-worn path to the west and to the northeast.

The path to the northeast is initially over rocky ground but eventually crosses boggy land where the route is difficult to follow and is often non existent. The direction from Cnoc an Bhráca is a few degrees to the right of the Strickeen Hill promontory, a peak that has the appearance of a windswept sand dune. However, three-quarters of the way over the bog, the path diverges to the east. This is an important point in the walk, for to miss this turn will take you over very steep and rough ground.

Under Strickeen is a blanket bog that has been worked to win turf for home heating. Remnants of the turf cutting can still be seen. From the blanket bog a track has been cut down to the Gap. This path zig-zags on a gentle gradient and was used to ferry the turf down from the plateau by donkey to the homes and farms below. The path is now the start of the Reeks Walk.

Of interest on the Turf Path is the enormous cliff face to the south which shows the rock formation with its horizontal bedding. Beyond the cliff there is a striking view up the Gap.

As you emerge onto the public road in the Gap of Dunloe you may care to note that the rocks on the valley floor have been rounded and scraped as the ice forced its way along the valley. The rocks at the junction of the Turf Path and the road are quartz conglomerate.

Walk Times: The walk through the Gap will take about one hour, possibly a little more if you are pausing to savour the atmosphere.

From the Gap up to Cnoc an Bhráca will take two hours.

The return down to Kate Kearney's is a one and a half hour journey.

Survival Tips: Of the two choices of where to begin the climb, to commence near Gap Cottage is the more straightforward. The initial climb up from the alternative, Head of the Gap, is quite safe but not as safe as a descent, hence the choice of direction. There are no paths for the first half of the walk. On the final leg of the walk a divergence too far to the east would take you dangerously close to the cliff face.

Good waterproof boots and gaiters are essential in the boggy ground. Some of the bog cuttings are very deep.

The summit of Cnoc na Tarbh

Walk 2

PURPLE MOUNTAIN

Summary: A challenging, safe walk through the Gap of Dunloe to the top of Purple Mountain, then on to Tomies Mountain, to descend into Dunloe Lower. If the day is clear there will be good views of the lakes of Killarney on one side and the Reeks on the other side.

Time: 5 to 6 hours   **Distance:** 14 km   **Ascent:** 900 m

Start and Finish: Kate Kearney's Cottage

Escape Routes: It is best to retreat the way you have come up.

Route Description   see **map 5** page **63**

This walk may be done in either a clockwise or anticlockwise direction. The walk through the Gap can be more pleasant in the early morning, when perhaps it will be more appreciated. A 6 km road walk at the end of the day may be somewhat boring.

Walk through the Gap of Dunloe, as for Walk 1 to the Head of the Gap. There is a clearly visible shoulder rising from the Head of the Gap which you will be taking. You may access it from the Head of the Gap or, alternatively, take a shortcut from the hairpin bends on the road.

Turn off the public road at **215:87082:83815** and walk up to the hairpin above. This brief shortcut from hairpin to hairpin is known as O'Donohoe's Steps.

From O'Donohoe's Steps follow a reasonably well trodden path up the mountain. There is a good view point over the Gap at a massive broken rock that is known as Madman's Rock (**300:87368:83697**). From Madman's Rock the direction is east until you reach the shoulder and the stream (**325:87475:83715**).

The route up is well defined. It follows a fence and a stream that are parallel. This will take you to Glas Lough, a picturesque perched lake, where a welcome break may be made as you look up to the summit of Purple Mountain. Note the way the rocks that bound the side of Glas Lough are folded. Was the mountain called Purple Mountain due to the colour of the rock, or was it due to the heather that grows over it? Why

The route around Glaslough towards Purple Mountain

might Glas Lough be called *Glasloch*, the green lake?

From Glas Lough proceed around the western shore and then swing around to the east, following the steep path. The path turns towards the summit of Purple and is then not so well defined. The simple direction is to head towards the summit over loose rock and scree. Purple Mountain has a long summit oriented SW – NE. There are several cairns, with not much difference in elevation between them.

Descending from Purple there is a cairn at **757:89445:85850** where it is necessary to turn to the north towards An Chathair. From here note that the rock underfoot is of the quartz conglomerate variety. Care is required over the rocks on the descent from An Chathair. Tomies Mountain is then north-northwest. Maintain this direction on the descent from Tomies down over steep heather, before swinging to the north. In the valley below there is a bright green shed towards which you are headed. Alternatively, if the mist is thick, proceed towards **259:88777:88449**, which is a point on the path down. The eventual goal is to walk on the western side of a fence down between furze and boulders to the dirt track at **114:88500:89500**. This dirt track takes you through gates out to the public road north of Kate Kearney's at **51:88145:89410**.

Above: *Madman's Rock overlooks the Head of the Gap at the upper end of the Gap of Dunloe. At the bend in the road below there is another rock that has a view down the Gap. This is known as Madman's Seat. Off to the left, just above the Head of the Gap, there is an isolated rock known as Gentleman's Rock*

Walk Times: From Kate Kearney's to the Head of the Gap is one hour, then the three next stages to Glas Lough, Purple and over to Tomies each take three-quarters of an hour to an hour. Then the descent back to Kate Kearney's is an hour and a half.

Survival Tips: This is a well-trodden route, not very difficult to follow. At the top of Purple proceed from cairn to cairn. After reaching Tomies descend initially to the northwest and then turn north. It is very important that you do not wander too far to the west after Tomies, since there are steep cliffs. From Tomies the direction to the exit is towards a bright green shed. There is no shortcut to Kate Kearney's, unless you are prepared to go through rough heather and cross the river.

The route up is wet and muddy so waterproof boots and gaiters are required. From the summit down it is much drier.

There is a difference between the 1:25,000 map and the 1:50,000 Map 78. An Chathair, at 735m, was formerly referred to as Tomies Mountain. The latter is now positioned at 568m elevation.

Map 5 - Purple Mountain

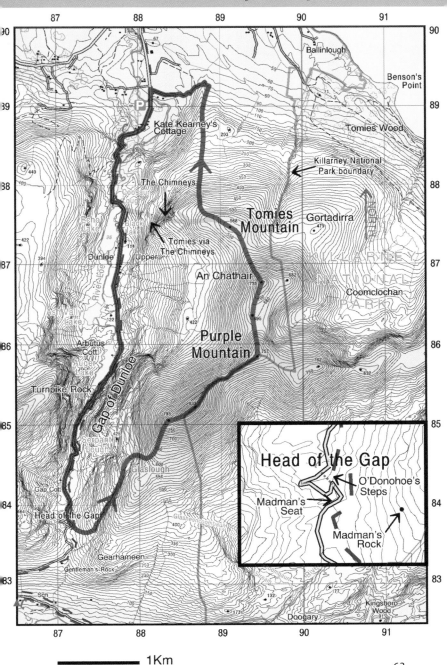

1Km

Walk 3

TOMIES VIA THE CHIMNEYS

Summary: This is an alternative route up to Tomies and Purple Mountain. It is a steep, though safe, climb through heather and loose rocks, eventually emerging at the top of a gully. In summertime you will hear the jarvies shouting as they bring their traps of tourists around Echo Lake directly below The Chimneys.

Time: From the Gap of Dunloe to the top of the Chimneys is 45 minutes. From Kate Kearneys to the top of Tomies Mountain is an ascent of 500 m. A walk from Kate Kearneys to Tomies, returning via the north, will be completed in under 3 hours.

Time: 3 to 4 hours   **Distance:** 3 km   **Ascent:** 500 m

Start and Finish: Kate Kearney's Cottage

Escape Routes: There are none. Descending this route is too steep.

Route Description   see **map 5** page **63**

The Chimneys are known locally as *Céim an Fhia*, the jump of the deer. There is a legend about the deer jumping from here over the Gap of Dunloe.

Walk into the Gap from Kate Kearney's, passing the small Black Lake, and cross the bridge at the next lake, Echo Lake.

You should look up from here at your route. Towards the centre of Tomies Rocks there are two distinct gullies, with a high chimney of rock between them. The climb is through the right-hand Gully.

Between where you are and The Chimneys there is a cliff escarpment. The route is to the left of this escarpment.

Immediately over the bridge at Echo Lake there is a gap in the fence at **100: 87710:87795** which is the start of the route. There is a narrow path but if you lose it, then your direction should be to the left of the cliff escarpment ahead. This is at **170:88042:87657**. The path zig-zags to the side of the escarpment, then passes over heather and loose rocks up to the gully.

It is possible to climb through any of the gullies, though the route through those other than the one we are describing can be gruelling. The base of the right-hand gully is at **275:88340:87600** and the top of the gully is at **425: 88410:87550**. The route through the gully is well defined.

These chimneys are cliffs of quartz conglomerate rock, which you may want to read about in the section on *Geology*.

From the top of The Chimneys the choices are to go to Tomies, An Chathair and Purple, returning through The Gap, or to go north from Tomies and return to Kate Kearney's via the green shed.

Survival Tips: There is a narrow path all the way up through the Chimneys. However, it is often difficult to find where it traverses over loose rock. Finding and following the path is less of a struggle than going though the thick heather. The climb is steep. Ground conditions are dry.

Left:
Tomies Chimneys

Above:
St Patrick's Cabbage is a popular wild flower especially on rocky ground

Walk 4

THE LOUGH GOOGH CIRCUIT

Summary: This walk could aptly be named 'The Waterfall Ascent to Knocknapeasta and Return over Derrycarna'. It is perhaps one of The Reeks most beautiful circuits, not very well documented heretofore. The route is over, or passing, numerous waterfalls. There are three options on this walk:

- upon arrival at Lough Googh, contour around and return via Doire Chearna Cumar;
- continue up from Lough Googh to Knocknapeasta, across the ridge to the Big Gun, and descend to Doire Chearna Cumar;
- from Knocknapeasta follow the ridge over to the Big Gun and on to Cruach Mhór, Cnoc an Bhráca, Cnoc na Tarbh, to descend to Gap Cottage.

Times: The circuit to Lough Googh is 3½ hours, one hour to the lake, one hour of a traverse and a little over an hour to return.

To Knocknapeasta and the Big Gun is a 5-hour trek and the longer circuit that returns via Gap Cottage is 6 hours. The ascent from Lúib an Bhóthair to Knocknapeasta is 850m.

Time: 3 to 6 hours   **Distance:** 8 to 12 km   **Ascent:** 850 m

Start and Finish: Beyond the Head of the Gap, in the Black Valley, at the first hairpin bend, Lúib an Bhóthair.

Escape Routes: It is possible to curtail the route short of the summit of Knocknapeasta and to descend to the east into a narrow valley above Lough Googh. By contouring around there is a way to descend to the shore of Lough Googh and retreat back following the river. The route is not, however, straightforward, so that returning the way one has ascended may be the safest option.

Route Description   see **map 6**

Drive through the Gap over into the Black Valley. The road drops to a hairpin bend. There are two parking spaces here, and a few more at the Head of the Gap. Directly at the hairpin bend, at **134:85840:83120** step

Map 6 - The Lough Googh Circuit and Cummeenapeasta

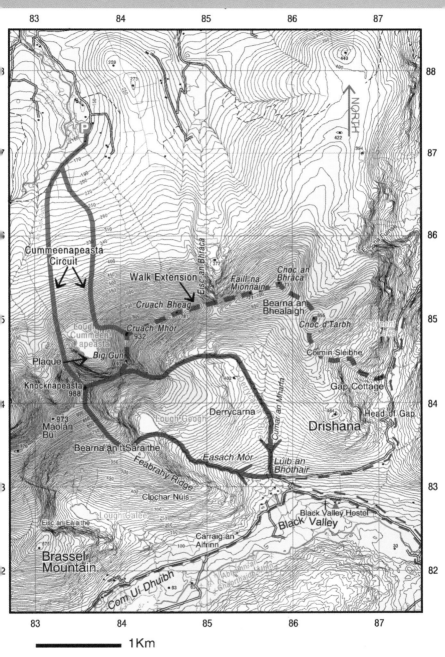

1Km

over the fence and go west towards an obvious waterfall. The hairpin bend is marked on the 1:25,000 map as *Lúib an Bhóthair*, which translates as *The Bend in the Road*.

There are many places to cross the wonderful waterfall, perhaps the safest and most picturesque is higher up under the tall pine trees. As you ascend to the west note the fine line of deciduous trees below you – birch, salix, mountain ash, whitethorn and holly – that follow the river. These trees support a thriving birdlife, where the cuckoo is a common visitor, and the woodland has not yet been invaded by the dreaded rhododendron. The name of Lough Googh comes from the Irish placename *Loch gCuach*, the lake of the cuckoo. I have visited this area in May on three consecutive years and each time heard the cuckoo. Indeed, on one occasion I saw a cuckoo. In May foxgloves and other wild flowers abound. On the peaty moorland delicate bog orchids and bog cotton may also be seen in early summer.

The ascent is to follow the river, with its many waterfalls, on a route west-northwest, to Lough Googh. There is an alternative route on the ridge above to the west, Feabrahy Ridge (*Fear Bréige*, the false man). Circle around Lough Googh to the west and ascend the obvious grass gully west of the lake. This gully is known as *Bearna an tSáraithe*, or *The Gap of the Surmounting*. At the top of the gully circle back to the north. On a clear day the summit of Knocknapeasta should be visible. This is attained over stony ground. Knocknapeasta is at **988:83590:84175**.

From Knocknapeasta to The Big Gun is over a narrow ridge. There is a well-defined path and it is necessary to cross from the north side to the south side of the ridge on occasions. The path that is lower down the ridge is safer than crossing the top of the ridge (though many will find the ridge traverse the more exhilarating).

If it is your intention to descend from The Big Gun, and not to continue to Cnoc na Bhráca, then it is not necessary to go to the top of The Big Gun but to contour around from the ridge until you meet an obvious gully to the southeast. This is at **895:84065:84440**. The way down is relatively steep but straightforward. A mountain trickle will develop into a stream and then into a river to fall into the valley below. There is one area where there is a waterfall and it is necessary to cross the river for a safe descent that is due southeast.

The terminal moraine under Drishana

You should be able to see the main river to your north, as it meanders around to meet your path. The river valley is known as *Doire Chearna Cumar*, translated as 'the riverbed of the oakwood of Kearney'. It cuts through the terminal moraine of gravel that was deposited during the ice age, when the glacier temporarily stopped and dropped its load of gravel under the Reeks.

Survival Tips: The ascent to Knocknapeasta is safe and reasonably direct. There is one steep grassy gully to negotiate. From Knocknapeasta to The Big Gun is over a ridge where it is necessary to be careful. It should be noted that traversing The Big Gun ridge in the west-to-east direction is not for the faint-hearted and may be too ambitious for the inexperienced walker. The ridge traverse is safest from east to west, can be dangerous in wet or icy weather, and in any event should not be attempted in windy conditions. The descent from the Big Gun is quite steep over grass and loose slabs of rock. The return to Derrycarna is also steep, over stony, then grassy ground.

This walk is not well known and you may not meet anybody except perhaps along the ridge. Underfoot the route is moderately wet in places. The rivers will need to be crossed on a number of occasions.

Safe Ascents and Descents on Carrauntoohil

SAFE ASCENTS AND DESCENTS ON CARRAUNTOOHIL

Carrauntoohil is not an easy mountain to climb. It is certainly not a safe mountain to climb. Like all mountains in this category it is generally much safer to ascend than it is to descend. In this chapter it is comparatively straightforward to list the ascent routes that an experienced hillwalker will have little difficulty with. However, to classify any of the descents as safe would be a misnomer.

During cold spells all routes up and down, other than perhaps those from the Black Valley (which faces south), will be prone to ice. Whereas the Zig-zags can be classified generally as a relatively safe route, under icy conditions it would be treacherous.

The following is a summary that displays the diversity of routes that are available, with notes on their relative safety. All of these routes are more fully described in the various walks.

The Devil's Ladder

The Devil's Ladder is the most popular route up and down the mountain, and as many as 60 per cent of those who climb Carrauntoohil take this path. The walk in to the ladder is relatively flat and presents few obstacles. So too is the steep walk up from the ladder to the summit cross.

The difficulty, and the danger, is on the ladder itself. This is a steep gully, filled with loose rocks, through which water constantly flows. Consequently there is a real danger at all times of rocks falling or sliding. The route description later in the book provides a list of 'do's' and 'don'ts' on the Devil's Ladder.

The Zigzags (Bóthar na Gíge)

To the east of the Devil's Ladder is a narrow path that provides a much safer route up and down. There is the same walk in and the same trudge up to the summit, the difference from the Ladder being that this is a

Above: *Warning sign at the top of Howling Ridge, near the summit of Carrauntoohil*
Previous page: *Looking down the Devil's Ladder*

steep, narrow path. It has the disadvantage that it is necessary to climb 100 m higher, then descend to the top of the Ladder, and the further disadvantage that it is very difficult to find either the bottom or the top of the Zig-zags. However, once you have discovered the path, the route is straightforward.

Under heavy snow the narrow path would be difficult to follow.

O'Shea's Gully

This is the second most popular route to the summit of Carrauntoohil and much more interesting than the Ladder. Going up there are three scramble steps to negotiate, facing in to the rock.

The O'Shea's route is complex, certainly not as straightforward as the Ladder or the Zig-zags. At the top of the Gully itself there is a sharp turn to the left and a scrambling ascent over boulders to the summit.

Heavenly Gates

The route in to Heavenly Gates is the same as for O'Shea's, with the same three steps to overcome. The ascent up to the Gates is a steep scramble but from there the path is safe.

Ascending Carrauntoohil via O'Shea's Gully and descending via Heavenly Gates is a popular round trip. Consequently, it is not advisable to ascend via Heavenly Gates in the afternoon. The Gates is a narrow passage, with scant room for those going up to pass those coming down. There is also the danger of falling stones from those descending.

Above: *Ascending to Lough Cummeenoughter.*
Right: *Steep descent at Heavenly Gates*

Map 7 - Ascents and Descents on Carrauntoohil

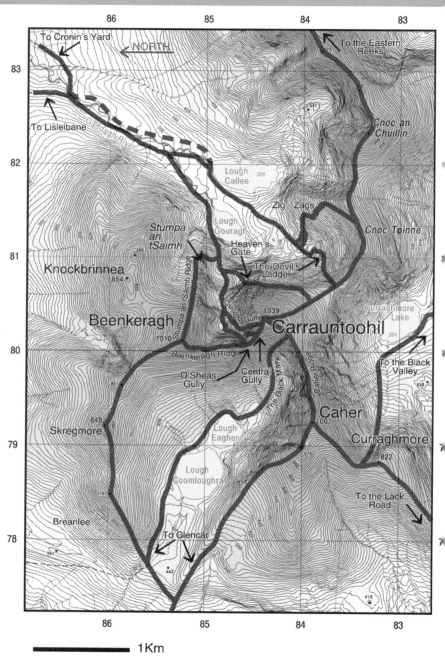

'The Bone' is a safe route up and down the Eastern Reeks

The Bone

The Bone is a very safe route up and down the Reeks. Where scrambling is opted for it is over relatively short distances and a fall on the Bone is unlikely to be as life threatening as elsewhere on the Reeks. The path on the Bone is well trodden and easy to find.

To get to the Bone unfortunately entails climbing and descending an additional 240 m and adds a further 7 km to the Devil's Ladder route.

Ascents from the Black Valley

There are a number of routes from the Black Valley up onto the Eastern Reeks and from there along the Reeks ridge over the top of the Devil's Ladder. These are not popular because there are few parking places in the Black Valley, there are no paths and descending back down into the Black Valley over steep grass can be very slippery.

A reasonable route is to drive into the Black Valley around Brassel Mountain and make an ascent up Capparoe to Cnoc an Chuillin, thence over the Eastern Reeks to Carrauntoohil.

The Black Mare Ascent from Glencar

This is a comparatively safe ascent but not at all suitable for descent. It is a kilometre more from Lough Acoose to the Black Mare than it is from Cronin's Yard or Lisleibane to The Devil's Ladder or the Zig-zags. The steepest part is over a grassy slope.

An ascent via the Black Mare and a descent via Caher is a relatively safe circuit.

Ascending Caher

The Caher Ascent from Glencar

To climb to Carrauntoohil via Caher is, like the Black Mare a longer route than those via Hag's Glen. There is the extra 20 km drive. It is necessary to go to the top of Caher, at 1001 m, and then descend below 900 m before climbing again to the 1039-metre cross. However, the route is comparatively safe. At the base there is no path and the ascent is over steep grass. Up on Caher there is a minor degree of scrambling.

The Caher Ascent from the Lack Road

The ascent and descent of Carrauntoohil via Caher and Curraghmore from the Lack Road is a safe and convenient route. There are two access points to the Lack Road, the first from Lough Acoose and the second from the Bridia Valley. It is a long drive around into the Bridia Valley and there are precious few parking places but this route is well worth suffering its disadvantages. Via Lough Acoose the drive is reduced and there are more places to park.

Routes via Beenkeragh

There is a narrow ridge from Beenkeragh to Carrauntoohil that should be reserved for the experienced hillwalker. It has been the scene of some casualties.

From Lisleibane it is a relatively straightforward climb to Beenkeragh

The curve on Curved Gully   *Central Gully*

via Knockbrinnea, the initial rise being over an unmarked grassy slope. The route from Knockbrinnea to the summit of Beenkeragh is a well-defined path, as it is again from Beenkeragh over the ridge to Carrauntoohil.

Beenkeragh may also be accessed from the Glencar side via Skregmore (see the Coomloughra Horseshoe).

There is a safe descent from Beenkeragh to Lisleibane via Knockbrinnea.

The Stumpa an tSaimh ridge climb to Beenkeragh is a relatively dangerous rock scramble in places and most unsuitable as a descent.

Curved and Central Gullies

These two gullies are merely variations on O'Shea's. Both are more dangerous that the Devil's Ladder. On no account should they be considered for descent.

Looking down to the top of the Devil's Ladder on Carrauntoohil. Those going to the left are heading for Heavenly Gates

Popularity of Routes

There is a long tradition of climbing Carrauntoohil on the day after Christmas Day (St. Stephen's Day in Ireland, Boxing Day in England). Hundreds converge on the Reeks to make the climb. It is interesting to examine the various routes that are used on this day.

On 26 December 2005 500 - 600 people climbed Carrauntoohil. There were over 100 cars parked in the Lisleibane area. By 10am there were no places to park either in Cronin's Yard, Lisleibane, the Black Valley or Glencar. The day was dry, with cloud cover at 900 m. It had not rained for a number of days and there was no snow or ice on the mountain.

The estimated breakdown of starting points was:
45 per cent at Lisleibane, 30 per cent at Cronin's Yard, 12 per cent at Glencar, 5 per cent in the Black Valley and 8 per cent elsewhere.

40 per cent ascended up the Devil's Ladder, another 35 per cent came via Heavenly Gates or O'Shea's, Curved or Central Gully, and 10 per cent came over Caher.

More descended the Devil's Ladder than ascended it. The second most popular descent was via Heavenly Gates. Not one climber ascended via the Zig-zags and only a handful descended via this route.

Hag's Glen Eastern Side

Walk 5

CUMMEENAPEASTA CIRCUIT

Summary: A short, though challenging walk into Hag's Glen, crossing the river and ascending up to a corrie lake. The route to the summit of Knocknapeasta is through boulders, where you may find the rusty remains of an aircraft that crashed in 1943. It may also be possible to see the wing of the aircraft glistening in the lake below.

From the summit there should be good views down into the Black Valley to the south and across to Carrauntoohil in the west. You have a choice of descents but the safest is down The Bone, accessed from the next peak to the west.

Time: 4 hours   **Distance:** 9 km   Ascent: 840 m

Start and finish: Cronin's Yard

Escape routes: Retracing one's steps down Knocknapeasta is steep but relatively safe.

The 1943 Crash of an American Dakota

In December 1943 twelve DC 3 transport planes took off from Fort Wayne in Indiana, USA, en route to England. They were intended to take an active part in the war. From the USA they had flown south to Brazil, then over to Ascension Island (St Helena) in the middle of the Atlantic, to Liberia in Africa and up to Marrakesh in Morocco. The last leg of the long journey was to be from Marrakesh into a small airfield near Mawgan in Cornwall.

Remnants of the propeller of the crashed Dakota on Knocknapeasta
Previous page: *The top of Devil's Ladder*

Three of the DC 3s had difficulties and did not set off from Morocco; the other nine left on the night of 16 December. Eight of the planes successfully landed in Cornwall but one never made it. On a bleak and stormy night it wandered off course and ended up over the Reeks. The five-man crew were all young men in their twenties – John Scharf, the pilot, Lawrence Goodin his co-pilot, and Vincent Brossard the navigator, were all recently married. They were supported by Arthur Schwartz, the radio operator and Wesley Holstaw, the engineer.

The plane crashed into the side of Knocknapeasta at 7am on the morning of 17 December. There was sleet and snow at the time; nobody was about and no report of any incident was made. It was not until 3 February that the crash was discovered and the army sent up to investigate. They brought the five bodies down and the American forces were informed. When the plane hit the mountain part of it fell into Lough Cummeenapeasta, part tumbled over the mountain onto the Black Valley side and some pieces were left on the mountain below Knocknapeasta.

In Cronin's Yard there is a memorial to the victims and at the Cummeenapeasta lakeside there is another commemorative plaque.

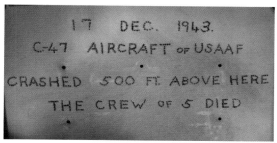

A simple plague at Lough Cummeenapeasta

Route Description

see **map 6** page **67**

Whilst this walk can use Lisleibane as a base Cronin's Yard has the advantage that the river does not have to be crossed. Leave Cronin's Yard by the well-trodden path, over a concrete footbridge, veering off the main farm path to the right to walk along beside the river into Hag's Glen, as far as the junction of the two rivers, then head towards Knocknapeasta. This is the second peak of the Reeks, the first, Cruach Mhór, distinguished by its prominent cairn.

Initially the route will be over bogland. If you divert up the mountain to the left too soon you will have to scale over the high bog cuttings. As you reach the base of the mountain the ground becomes firmer and you have to walk around boulders. There is no path up to the corrie lake of Lough Cummeenapeasta. The lakeside is a very pleasant place to stop for a breather. It is necessary to go around the lakeshore to the right to find the commemorative plaque. It is on the southwestern side of the lake, set into a rock outcrop.

From the plaque retrace your steps to where there is a vague path to the left up to the summit. The path hugs close to the southwestern edge of the lake. It is often over large boulders, where scrambling is required. You can divert to the edge and look down into the lake below to see the wing of the plane. This will only be visible on clear, sunny days.

At an altitude of 800 m you should begin to look out for the rusty remnants of the plane. When they were last located they were at **821:83440:84440**. The summit is not far. The small lake below on the Black Valley side is Lough Googh.

Having achieved the summit of Knocknapeasta you now have to decide on whether to go left to Cruach Mhór or to go right to the Bone. From Knocknapeasta around to Cruach Mhór is a ridge scramble over large boulders and along narrow ledges. The pinnacle of rocks between Knocknapeasta and Cruach Mhór is the Big Gun. Along these ridges the emphasis should be on care and safety, rather than on speed. If your choice is to go to the Bone you nevertheless must cross a ridge but the route is then not as daunting as that over the Big Gun.

The descent back down into Hag's Glen from Cruach Mhór is steep and must be carried out slowly, initially over large boulders, heading first to the shore of Lough Cummeenapeasta.

Survival Tips: Whilst there is a vaguely marked route up to Knocknapeasta and a well marked route down the Bone, the route over the flatter areas of the boggy base are not defined.

During the summer this route will be relatively dry. This is not a suitable walk for the inexperienced during icy conditions.

Walk 6

CARRAUNTOOHIL VIA THE DEVIL'S LADDER

Summary: This is the most popular route to the summit of Carrauntoohil. It is not the safest route but it is the most straightforward.

From Cronin's Yard or from Lisleibane it is a relatively flat walk to the base of the Devil's Ladder. Up the Ladder it is a scramble through a wide gully that has loose boulders. From the top of the Ladder to the summit is a long and arduous trudge on a well-defined path through rocks.

Time: The average time over the route up can be subdivided into one hour to the base of the Ladder, one hour on the Ladder and a further hour to the summit. The round trip therefore can be achieved in about 5 hours.

Time: 5 hours   **Distance:** 13 km   **Ascent:** 900 m

Start and Finish: The most popular parking area is Cronin's Yard but Lisleibane has grown in popularity over recent times. The road into Lisleibane, at the time of writing, is rough and has many deep potholes, whereas the Cronin's Yard road does not have these obstacles. At Cronin's Yard there are changing rooms, showers and there is a small café. A nominal charge is made to park at Cronin's Yard.

Whether from Lisleibane or Cronin's Yard it is necessary to cross the river. However, there are quite safe crossing places on either route.

Escape Routes: There are no escape routes on this climb. The only option is to retrace your steps.

Route Description   see map 8 page 87

From Cronin's Yard pass the memorials on the wall and go through gates along a fenced path, over a concrete footbridge and into the Hag's Glen. If the weather is clear you will see, starting on your left, the mountain with the pimple, Cruach Mhór. Directly ahead, towards the southwest, the lower of the two cols that can be seen is the top of the Devil's Ladder. To the right of it the sharp outline of Carrauntoohil may be visible.

The path will cross a tributary river at **190:83050:86545** from which the trail rises and there is a choice of paths. Take the right-hand path

Crossing the river in the Hag's Glen

that goes down by the river. You will soon need to make a decision as to whether to cross the river or not. If the river is not in flood you should cross, because the trail is simpler to follow from the other side. The most popular point to cross is at **225:82715:86400**. Here there is an island in the middle of the river that divides the flow, and there is a little mountain ash tree growing on the island.

After crossing the river rise to the upper bank and follow the stony path all the way to the Devil's Ladder. The stony path crosses back over the river again but at a place where there are plenty of stepping stones.

If the river is in flood do not cross but continue along the eastern bank. The path leaves the river for a stretch and then eventually comes back to it. Where the river flows out of Lough Callee there is a wide expanse of flat rocks where a crossing is easy. This is near a popular area to camp, with rough coordinates **81945:84985**. You can rejoin the main path immediately to the west.

From Lisleibane take the left-hand gate. You may turn a sharp left and follow a well-defined track or climb directly ahead, over boulders and through ferns, the latter being a shortcut that rejoins the track near **235:82790:87000**. The track is a wide stony path that leads up through the Hag's Glen, crossing the river at a shallow part, and follows directly to the base of the Devil's Ladder.

At the base of the Devil's Ladder the well-defined track gives way to ill-defined muddy paths. The Ladder may be considered in three phases

– the lower, wet boulder area, the middle stony scree section that is quite wide, and the narrow upper section.

The greatest danger posed on the ladder is that of falling rocks from above. This is less of a risk on the middle, wider section than on the upper or lower sections.

'Do's and 'Don't's on the Devil's Ladder

- The most treacherous areas are near the base or towards the top, so try to save any long rests for the middle section.
- People climb the Ladder in the late morning and descend in the middle of the afternoon. Do not climb the Ladder, especially on a Sunday, in the middle afternoon.
- If there are other climbers close to you try to stick close with them, or give them some distance. If they are twenty metres or so above you, there is a greater likelihood of them causing a rockslide that will endanger you.
- The safest areas on the Ladder are close to the sides. It will not always be feasible to climb on only one side and there will be times when it is necessary to cross the Ladder. Do not linger unnecessarily in the middle of the gully.
- If you notice rocks that are obviously so loose as to pose a danger lift them and place them so that the danger is removed.
- If you accidentally knock a rock and it is falling, with people in danger below you, the recognised call is **'below'**. If you need to make this call make it loudly and immediately.

At the top of the Ladder the path narrows and is relatively soft and slippery, and endless feet have cut a deep ravine in the gully. As you emerge onto the col be careful of the wind, especially on the slippery, muddy ground. The route is to the right.

From the top of the Ladder it is a long trudge over stony paths to the summit. All the paths lead to the same place. The top of Ireland is marked by a high steel cross. Around its base there are a number of rock enclosures that give limited shelter.

The steel cross on the summit of Carrauntoohil was erected by Beaufort Community Council in 1975. It replaced a wooden cross that the council mounted on the summit in 1950

On the return journey, if you are heading for Cronin's Yard, the point at which you leave the path to go down to the river is at **240:82700:86430**.

Survival Tips: The route to the Ladder is generally wet – whether it is crossing the river or through muddy patches at the base of the Ladder – so that waterproof boots are essential.

Please read the list of 'Do's and 'Don't's for the Devil's Ladder.

Map 8 - The Devil's Ladder, the Zig-zags and the Bone

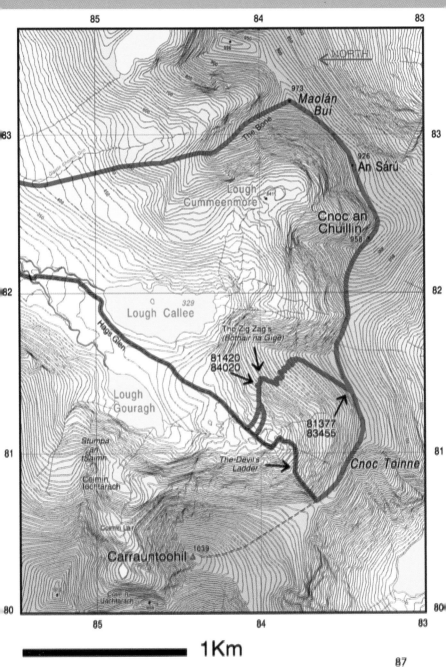

1Km

Walk 7

UP THE ZIG-ZAGS *(BÓTHAR NA GÍGE)* AND DOWN THE BONE

Summary: This walk is probably the safest ascent and descent on the Reeks. It is the route used by the locals for materials access – the summit cross was taken up this route. The Zig-zags is close to the Devil's Ladder and is a narrow path that ascends up the flank of the area west (or to the left) of the Ladder. It is not a popular route, possibly because it is not easy to find, but is a much safer ascent or descent than the Devil's Ladder.

The Bone similarly can be used either as an ascent or a descent and is a recognised escape route on the eastern Reeks.

Time: 3½ to 4½ hours   **Distance:** 14 km   **Ascent:** 930 m

Start and Finish: Cronin's Yard or Lisleibane.

Escape Routes: Both the ascent and the descent are most suitable as escape routes.

Route Description   see **map 8** page **87**

Follow the route from either Lisleibane or Cronin's Yard into Hag's Glen (see Carrauntoohil via the Devil's Ladder) and in towards the base of the Devil's Ladder. There is no cairn or landmark to define the start of the Zig-zags, so that you will have to adopt some initiative. As you follow the river you should be aware of a wide ledge on your left that gradually rises to the east. To get to this ledge requires you to climb over grassy ground between rock outcrops. If you have a GPS you will be leaving the river anywhere between **452:81130:84070** and **453:81110:84030** to go east. Your direction is towards **543:81420:84020** where you should be able to pick up the base of the path.

The narrow path is initially a gentle rise over grass to the east. It gradually changes into a series of zig-zags to the south and southeast, before it eventually takes a long sweep towards the southwest.

Finding the Top of the Zig-Zags

The top of the Zig-zags is at **827:81377:83455**. Once again there is no cairn or marker. If you have decided to descend the Zig-zags and are coming

Ascending the Zig-zags (Bóthar na Gíge)

east from the top of the Devil's Ladder these are the instructions:

Climb the first rise after the Ladder and walk over a relatively flat plateau. Halfway over the plateau, and before you reach a rock outcrop on your left, you should be able to see the narrow path below you.

Towards the Bone

From the top of the Zig-zags the trail is east, up to Cnoc an Chuillin at 958m, then over to the northeast to Maolán Buí at 973m. You will have circled around a small corrie lake – Lough Cummeenmore. Since there is

Looking towards Cnoc Toinne from *Maolán Buí*, with its yellow colour in autumn

a series of these hilltops, it is important to be sure that you are at the top of Maolán Buí. This has a GPS reference of **973:83207:83825**.

The Irish word, *maolán*, means flat hill, whilst *buí* means yellow. With the distinctive yellow colour of the grasses and mosses on this hill it is not difficult to see why it was so named.

The route down the Bone is north-northwest from Maolán Buí. There is a rusted steel post in the ground to mark the top of the Bone. The path is reasonably well defined, though on the flatter parts there are choices of which boulders to circumnavigate.

Emerging at the base of the Bone there should be an obvious spine heading directly north. To take this spine will shorten the journey which is otherwise to follow the Bone all the way towards the northwest and the tip of Lough Callee.

Survival Tips: The Zig-zags is a narrow path that may be impossible to follow if there is a covering of snow. It would also be unsafe without crampons in icy conditions. Locating the top and the bottom of the Zig-zags is difficult (hence the precise instructions above).

Hag's Glen Western Side

Walk 8

CARRAUNTOOHIL VIA O'SHEA'S GULLY RETURNING BY HEAVENLY GATES

Summary: This route is the most popular circuit made by experienced hillwalkers. It has the advantage of being relatively safe and direct and there will generally be other trekkers if you get into trouble. Following an undulating walk over rough ground the route rises steeply, with occasional scrambling. Emerging at a col the final phase to the summit is over large boulders. On the return there is a section of steep descent through a gully before rejoining the inward path.

This is a most interesting way to climb Carrauntoohil. It is at times challenging and crosses diverse terrain. You will pass the mountain refuge on the return journey. This is a grass-covered building, and is complete with beds, food and water.

Time: For a reasonably fit person, who has little difficulty following this route, and allowing times to appreciate the views, have lunch on the summit, the time should be between 5 and 6 hours.

Time: 5 to 6 hours   **Distance: 14½ km**   **Ascent: 900m**

Start and Finish: Lisleibane or Cronin's Yard

Escape Routes: There are no escape routes. Should the weather change or an incident occur on the ascent of O'Shea's Gully then it is possible to descend the Gully and return by the same route. If the path to Heavenly Gates cannot be located it may be necessary to descend via the Devil's Ladder.

Route Description   see **map 9** page **97** and **map 7** page **74**

From Cronin's Yard follow the same route into Hag's Glen as for the Zig-zags or the Devil's Ladder. Cross the river at **210:82715:86400** and rise to the upper road.

From Lisleibane take the central gateway. You may walk along the flat road that leads off to the left or take a shortcut up the mound directly in front, eventually joining the road at **235:82790:87000**.

Follow the stony road as far as **290:82125:85455**. On your right you will have passed the Hag's Small Teeth but you will not have yet arrived at the Large Tooth. You will not be far from the river. Do not cross the river. Here it is necessary to leave the road and to take a route to the right and west of Lough Gouragh. There is no defined path. Around the base of the Hag's Tooth you should find one of two paths; both lead to where you are heading. One of these is at **330:81820:85280**.

On the path up around the base of the Hag's Tooth it is necessary to go around, rather than climb, a rock promontory at **380:81585:85030**. There are a number of steps to climb, the first of which is at **420:81200:84955**, and the third, and final step is under Stumpa an tSaimh at **475:81020:84835**. These steps are known as *Na Teanntaí*, the steps, or the supports. The path becomes steeper before it emerges into a boggy flat section at **530:80900:84850**. We will refer to this as Level 1, *Cummeeneighter*, the lower little coom. This is the junction of the route up and the route down, and you may want to become acquainted with it.

Follow the path directly west; it rises and leads over bare rock, flattens to Level 2, *Cummeenlour*, the middle little coom, and rises again to a corrie lake, Lough *Cummeenoughter*, at Level 3, **740:80350:84810**, upper little coom. Along the southern side of the lake the route turns south to

Route up O'Shea's Gully indicated by dotted line; entrance to Curved Gully arrowed

rise steeply up O'Shea's Gully, which is now on a southwest course. This is the most strenuous part of the ascent.

Before you leave the corrie lake of Cummeenoughter take a look at the outline of the geological fault. The line is from Central Gully high up on your left, across the cliff that forms the north shore of the lake, and proceeds to cut into the mountain on the far side under Beenkeragh. Along the line of the fault there is a displacement of over 100 m, the land on the east having been displaced southwards.

The likelihood is that the three gullies, Curved, Central and O'Shea's, are all related to the fault, when a general shattering of the area occurred. The three gullies converge towards the Black Cliff at the northern edge of Lough Cummeenoughter.

O'Shea's Gully was named after a Brother O'Shea, who died in 1968 after falling in the gully. Locally it is referred to as *Brother O'Shea's Gully*. At the top of the gully you will emerge at a col on the path from Beenkeragh to Carrauntoohil, at **920:80085:84555**. Turn left, to the east, and climb to the summit (**1039:80365:84425**).

The Descent

Leave the summit cross, descending with your back to it, and take the obvious well-trodden path down the mountain heading southeast. At **820:80460:84000** turn to the east, following the contours. Your bearing is towards **780:80620:83935**, the start of the path to Heavenly Gates. The path begins at a point left of a cluster of large boulders. It is important to find this path, since any other route in this direction would be too steep. Once you have discovered the path the route becomes very clear. This path is known as the ramp.

Heavenly Gates (**740:80700:84525**) is a narrow opening between the rock faces above a steep gully. From Heavenly Gates Howling Ridge rises to the summit of Carrauntoohil, a popular climb requiring ropes and harnesses.

You should put away walking poles and prepare yourself for this steep descent. In places it may be necessary to come down on your backside.

At the base of the gully where the trail flattens is the mountain refuge. At **580:80822:84660** the stone structure with its earthen roof, blends naturally into the landscape. You may enter the tunnel and open the door; stand up inside the snug, dark interior; it has bunk beds and is regularly stocked with food; outside there is a water tap. This area is known as The Eagle's Nest.

The path becomes steep again and descends over boggy ground to cross a stream and joins the route up to O'Shea's Gully. As you descend from here you will have to negotiate the rock steps that you climbed on the way up. These steps are prone to accidents, so take care; put away walking poles; descend backwards; locate good handgrips.

Heavenly Gates. These walkers are about to descend through them

Survival Tips: There are a number of places where it is necessary to climb over solid rock faces and to descend over the same faces. There are good foot steps and hand holds but you should be used to descending backwards, facing into the rock face. In the winter the upper parts of this route are prone to ice: it is on the north face of the mountain. In these circumstances crampons and/or an ice-axe may be necessary.

On the route in there is a section after you leave the river that is ill-defined and has no path. Adopt the principle of staying low, rather than climbing too early. For the descent finding the path towards Heavenly Gates from the summit is not so easy.

There are parts of the route over boggy ground where waterproof boots and gaiters are essential.

Map 9 - O'Shea's, Curved and Central Gullies, Heavenly Gates

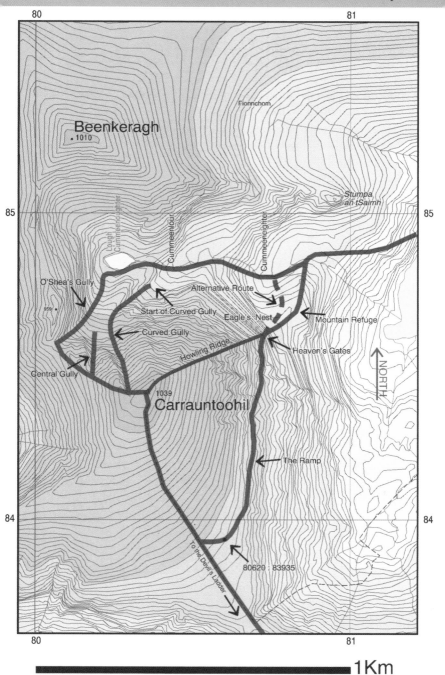

1Km

Walk 9

CARRAUNTOOHIL VIA CURVED GULLY OR CENTRAL GULLY

Summary: This is a variation on the route up O'Shea's Gully. It involves steep scrambling through a gully that is strewn with loose rock. Curved Gully emerges almost at the summit of Carrauntoohil. From the summit there are many choices of descent including Heavenly Gates or the Zig-zags.

Central Gully is a similar gully to Curved Gully and is immediately west of it. Some climbers enter Curved Gully and leave it at its curve to climb up Central Gully.

Time: 4½ to 5½ hours   **Distance:** 14 km   **Ascent:** 900m

Start and Finish: Lisleibane or Cronin's Yard

Escape Routes: See Carrauntoohil via O'Shea's Gully and Heavenly Gates.

Route Description   see **map 9** page **97**

Proceed in through Hag's Glen and climb up towards O'Shea's Gully. Before the last climb to Lough Cummeenoughter, at **675:80440:84820** on the flat ground of Cummeenlour, it is possible to look up to Curved Gully. It is a narrow gully and generally has water flowing out of it. O'Shea's Gully is a wide gully to the right, running almost parallel. The entrance to Curved Gully is at **760:80300:84700**.

The initial entrance is a high step over a large boulder that has water flowing over it. If this is too difficult or if the water is too much then you may proceed around the rock escarpment to the right and enter the gully further up.

The purists climb Curved Gully following the water all the way to the top. This is a formidable route, precarious in places. It is more customary to occasionally leave the gully to avoid the steeper steps.

Central Gully is not quite as steep and not as full of loose boulders as Curved Gully.

The top of both gullies is a steep grassy slope. It is here that a rope or crampons may be needed on icy mornings. The exit from Curved Gully is onto the path from Beenkeragh and O'Shea's Gully, and the

Ascending Curved Gully

summit cross can be seen around to the left. The exit from Central Gully is considerably lower down and it is necessary to scramble and climb to reach Curved Gully exit.

WALK TIMES: Very similar to O'Shea's Gully, perhaps a gain of half an hour.

Survival Tips: The initial entry to Curved Gully is over a high rock that is usually quite wet – often in fact a waterfall.

After the first section of Curved Gully it is possible to leave the gully and return to the O'Shea's Gully route, or to take the route via Central Gully. However, once you have started into either of the upper gullies the only option is to proceed to the top. Descending down one of these gullies is not an option.

Never climb Curved Gully or Central Gully on your own. If you become trapped by falling rocks you may not be able to raise the alarm. Always bring a rope of at least ten metres in length. If you are in a group restrict the number to five or six and keep the group close together. If there are climbers ahead you have the option of going out of Curved Gully and up through Central Gully.

It is quite easy to dislodge loose rocks, which can cause an avalanche. The common warning, when a rock has been dislodged is to shout *'below'.*

Map 10 - Stumpa An tSaimh and the Beenkeragh Ridge

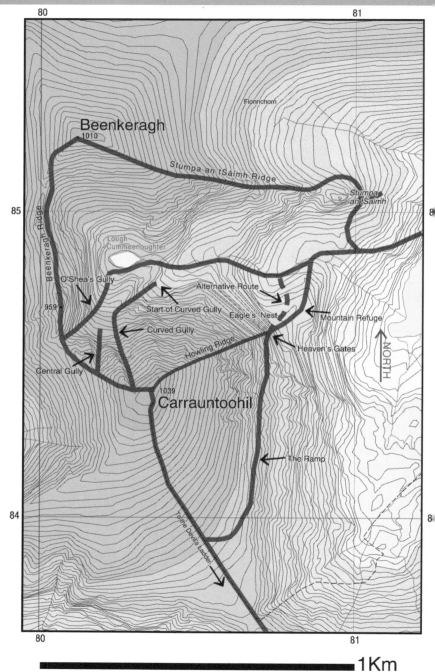

Beenkeragh
1010

Stumpa an tSaimh Ridge

Stumpa an tSaimh

Beenkeragh Ridge

Lough Cummeenoughter

O'Shea's Gully

Alternative Route

Start of Curved Gully

Eagle's Nest

Mountain Refuge

Curved Gully

Howling Ridge

Heaven's Gates

959

Central Gully

Carrauntoohil
1039

NORTH

The Ramp

To the Devil's Ladder

1Km

Walk 10

STUMPA an tSAIMH RIDGE TO BEENKERAGH

Summary: This is a scrambling route directly up to the summit of Beenkeragh. Although it is not for the faint hearted, the route is not technical and does not require ropes.

From Beenkeragh choices are available to traverse the Beenkeragh Ridge to Carrauntoohil or to descend via Knockbrinnea.

Time: 5 hours   **Distance:** 11 km   **Ascent:** 870m

Escape Routes: Retracing your steps back down is a reasonable option, though one that requires some care. It is also possible, with care, to contour across to Knockbrinnea.

Route Description   see **map 10** opposite

Follow the route for O'Shea's Gully, scaling the three steps and arriving at Level 1 at **530:80930:84860**. This is the point where the route up to O'Shea's meets the route down from Heavenly Gates. Immediately above you to the north is the Stumpa an tSaimh peak. It is pronounced *Stumpa an Sawve*. Many walkers and climbers may (mistakenly) refer to this peak as The Hag's Tooth.

Climb up to the north and circle around the base of the peak on its eastern side. From here there is a steep, grassy gully that will take you up to the ridge. Having gained the ridge the summit of Beenkeragh is due west.

You have the choice of how difficult a scramble you wish to pursue. The purists will want to follow the ridge all the way, whilst walkers may want to avoid the dangers of some of the exposed areas.

As you approach Beenkeragh there is a large boulder field before reaching the summit.

The Descent

From Beenkeragh the safest descent is via Knockbrinnea. This is over relatively steep ground, stony to begin with, and over a clear path, then grassy, with no path down over heather.

From Beenkeragh towards Knockbrinnea the route is northeast. There

is no defined path over the boulders around the summit. However, once you are headed in the general northeast direction there is little danger. If the mist impairs visibility then keep descending to the northeast or set a course for Knockbrinnea at **854:80765:85815**. Eventually a path over the rocky ground will appear.

En route to Knockbrinnea, in the col area shown on the Ordnance map as *Glóras*, you may see a distinctive rock feature. Known as 'Aircraft Rock', its recognition may boost your confidence of being on the correct route.

Survival Tips: There are exposed areas of the ridge where accidents occur. However, these exposed and dangerous areas can be bypassed.

Above left: *Stumpa an tSaimh (Stumpeenadaff) is often referred to as the Hag's Tooth*

Above right:
The gully behind Stumpa an tSaimh

Right:
Aircraft rock under Beenkeragh

Walk 11

BEENKERAGH VIA CUMMEENAGEARAGH

Summary: To climb to the top of Carrauntoohil is a great experience, but to see Carrauntoohil in all its splendour there is no better vantage point than Beenkeragh. This walk is in a quiet area of the Reeks, seldom frequented by other walkers. There is a choice of a gentle climb through heather and over boulders or a more challenging scramble through a steep gully.

Time: From the parking place to the summit of Beenkeragh is **2½ to 3 hours.**

Distance: 4 km (ascent only)   **Ascent: 950m**

Start: This walk may commence at the Lisleibane car park. However, a better starting point is further west in Knockroe. The directions are simple: after you have turned off the Glencar Road, onto the Lisleibane Road, instead of turning up to the left for Lisleibane after the narrow concrete bridge, continue travelling due west to the end of the dirt track road. Ask for permission to park and to travel over the farmer's land.

Route Description   see **map** 11 page **113**

At the end of the dirt track road there is a farm yard, with a farm track heading west that crosses the river. This is at **160:81340:88080**. Cross the river and enter a levelled, cultivated field. The route is directly across this field but you may have to go around the field to avoid damage to crops. The route is southwest, over rough ground between two rivers.

Cummeenagearagh is quite a distinct mountain corrie that should be easily distinguishable in the distance. The trail follows the river on the left that issues from the corrie.

As you ascend you must decide whether you will enter the corrie and climb the steep gully, or whether to climb the flank of the corrie to the right. Once you have entered the corrie there are only two obvious routes up the mountain, the gully or a steep scree slope. The gully is very similar to Curved Gully. It has one high step but this can be by-passed by climbing up to the right. The high step is in the darkest section of the gully.

Within the gully St Patrick's Cabbage is abundant, particularly near the top. There is one section of the gully where there is a natural shower, as water from the rock sprays over the gully.

The alternative walking route to avoid the gully is a gentle climb, initially over heather, then boulders, to the summit of Stuaic Bharr na hAbhann (the peak of the top of the river) at **851:79640:85880**.

From Stuaic Bharr na hAbhann or the top of the gully to the summit of Beenkeragh is due south-southeast, another half an hour away.

From Beenkeragh the choices of further walking are numerous – cross the Beenkeragh Ridge to Carrauntoohil and return via Heavenly Gates and Lisleibane, descend via Knockbrinnea, or, if you have climbed the Cummeenagearagh gully, you may descend from Stuaic Bharr na hAbhann.

Right: *The Gully at Cummeenagearagh*
Over: *The Coomloughra Lakes from the Beenkeragh Ridge*

Routes from Glencar

Walk 12

THE COOMLOUGHRA HORSESHOE

Summary: There are few walks in any country that can rival the Coomloughra Horseshoe and this is certainly the finest walk in Ireland. It can be a long, arduous day traversing over the three highest peaks in Ireland. The walk is 12 km in length and follows a series of ridges that circle the Coomloughra Lakes. There are dangerous traverses to be made over exposed ridges, some scrambling and a degree of navigation on overcast days. The walk is not suitable on windy days.

Time: 6 to 7 hours   **Distance:** 12 km   **Ascent:** 1200m

Start: There are two choices of start and finish – Lough Acoose or the Concrete Road. There is also the choice of walking clockwise around the circuit, or anti-clockwise.

Escape Routes: From Skregmore to Beenkeragh it is possible to descend with care into the Coomloughra Valley. From Beenkeragh around to Caher there are no such escape routes into Coomloughra but there are safe routes towards the Devil's Ladder and Curraghmore.

Route Description   see **map 11** page **113**

From either of the two possible starting points the first objective is the dam at Lough Eighter. This is the most northerly of the three Coomloughra lakes. Whether you park at Lough Acoose or near the Concrete Road, it will take half an hour to get to Lough Eighter.

The Concrete Road, also known as the Hydro Road, is a rough concrete path. Under the path there is a one-metre diameter pipe that conveys water from the Coomloughra Lakes to generate electricity in a small generating station below. A business company in Macroom acquired the rights to the system but the current owner of the land, a farmer in Knockroe, receives no income from the scheme. In 1990 the electricity being generated had a value of over €1000 per day. The construction of the dam and the pipeline has been the source of much criticism and controversy. Environmentalists have maintained that it is a scar on the landscape in that it could have been constructed with more sensitivity.

Start of the Beenkeragh Ridge near Beenkeragh

The Concrete Road starts at a wooden fence and gateway at **130:77170:87050**. There is a Kerry Mountain Rescue sign beside the gateway. It is not easy to find a parking space near the gateway. There is a disused quarry on the approach to the Concrete Road but signs clearly preclude parking at the wooden gateway. From the gateway there is an obvious route up to the dam at Lough Eighter. The route is clearly marked as a dotted line on the Ordnance maps.

For the Lough Acoose starting point you turn off the main road to Glencar onto the road south around the lake. Within a half kilometre of the turn off find a safe parking place before a gate that blocks the road. There is no path from here to Lough Eighter – it is simply a case of striking off directly east, avoiding obvious high ground and you will eventually meet the Concrete Road. Point **310:76940:85467** has a fence you can follow that avoids the high ground. If you follow this for 300 m you can turn left and head northeast.

Lough Eighter is at **348:77760:85585**. The ascent to Skregbeg begins at the western end of the lake on a route northeast. There is a path through the heather that will make the route easier to follow once you find it. The word skreg comes from the Irish *screig*, meaning a rocky place.

The trail ascends to the first of the day's peaks at 747m, though there is little point in going off the path to this summit. The path is lower down on the Coomloughra Glen side. The next peak is Skregmore, where the path begins to turn to the southeast.

At Beenkeragh there is a scramble over boulders to the summit. On a clear day the Beenkeragh Ridge will be visible directly south. There are three routes from Beenkeragh summit to the ridge. By far the safest is the path on the eastern side, that facing Carrauntoohil. This avoids a scramble over the boulders that form the ridge. There is another path on the western side. To access this path, it is necessary to come down off the summit to the west, heading back towards Skregmore. The path is quite low down.

The Beenkeragh Ridge is known locally as *The Bone*, and fatalities have occurred with people falling off it.

You may notice that the ridge path is strewn with small white pebbles. These are quartz stones that have weathered out of the quartz conglomerate. Ice has split the rock and the hard quartz stones have popped out.

Be particularly careful of the ridge in windy conditions. There are two points where the path goes over a col and the slopes on either side are precipitous. The wind velocity in the col is higher, with obvious dangers.

After emerging from the ridge the path will pass by the tops of O'Shea's Gully, then Central Gully, and finally Curved Gully. There is some scrambling from O'Shea's Gully to Curved Gully; thereafter the path flattens and the cross of Carrauntoohil will be a welcome site.

From Carrauntoohil retrace your steps to Curved Gully where there is an obvious alternative path off to the left and south. This is the route to the Caher Ridge. Alternatively from the summit of Carrauntoohil the direction to Caher is south-southwest. The Caher Ridge, unlike the Beenkeragh Ridge, is initially relatively flat. It gradually forms into a humpback as it traverses over Caher. Be prepared for the last climb of

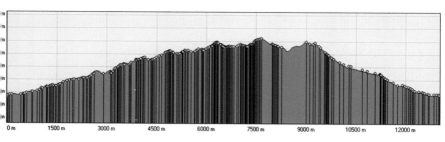

Profile of the Coomloughra Horseshoe trail using OSI's 'Trailmaster'

the day on Caher's third summit, at **975:78970:84006**.

The descent off Caher is a well-worn trail that is very safe and quite long. If you have parked at Lough Acoose you can leave the trail to strike off in a west-northwest direction or return via Lough Eighter.

Walk Times: It is half an hour from either starting point to Lough Eighter. From Lough Eighter to Beenkeragh is one and a half to two hours. The Beenkeragh Ridge to Carrauntoohil will take three-quarters of an hour, and a further three-quarters of an hour to the second summit of Caher. Expect the descent back to the start of the walk to take one and a half to two hours.

Survival Tips: The route clockwise is recommended, for a number of reasons, one being that the descent off Caher is safer than the descent off Skregmore. However, some will advise that the anti-clockwise route takes the climber to Carrauntoohil sooner, allowing one to retrace their steps if the weather or fatigue set in.

There are few areas to park near the Concrete Road and parking near Lough Acoose offers better possibilities.

From Beenkeragh there is a significant descent to the path for the Beenkeragh Ridge. The most dangerous part of the walk is the area of the Beenkeragh Ridge closest to Carrauntoohil. Caher has three summits, all of them on the path.

The route is at times over a combination of bogland, heather and rock. Occasionally the path is ill defined, so you will have to be alert.

Walk 13

THE BLACK MARE ASCENT TO CARRAUNTOOHIL

Summary: This is a relatively straightforward and safe route to the summit of Carrauntoohil. It begins with a walk up a concrete path, then circles the Coomloughra Lakes to make a steep climb through a wide, grassy gully, emerging within 100 m in elevation from the summit.

Time: 2 to 3 hours ascent Distance: 5½ km (ascent only) Ascent: 900m

Start: From either Lough Acoose or the base of the concrete road (see the Coomloughra Horseshoe).

Escape Routes: Once you have entered the Black Mare Gully there is little alternative but to continue to the summit ridge. The incline is too steep to descend.

Starting the ascent of the Black Mare

Route Description

see **map 11** opposite

Follow either of the routes to the dam at Lough Eighter (see the Coomloughra Horseshoe).

Circle Lough Eighter on its eastern shore and proceed eastwards to circle the shores of Lough Coomloughra and Lough Eagher. At the south-east end of Lough Eagher follow the river that rises steeply up the

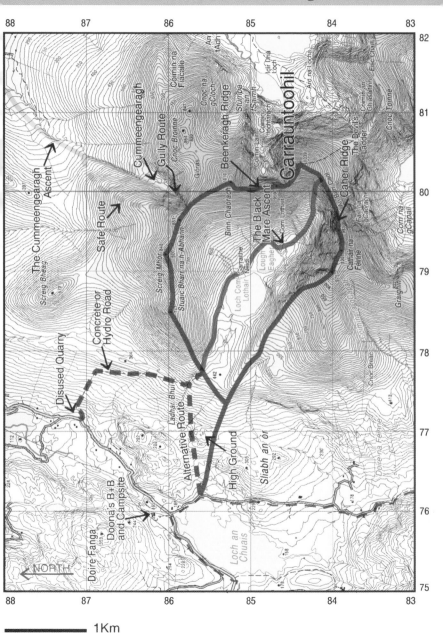

1Km

Caher Ridge in snow

mountain, passing through a number of terminal moraines – deposits of gravel during the ice ages where the ice stopped. It is immaterial which side of the river you climb. At a point **850:80090:84232** this wide gully subdivides into three narrower gullies. All of these lead to the summit ridge, possibly the most northern (left side) being the more straightforward.

At the summit ridge follow a well defined path over rocks to the summit of Carrauntoohil, which is less than fifteen minutes away.

The most obvious descent is via Caher – see Walk 12.

Survival Tips: From the end of the concrete road at the Lough Eighter dam there are no paths to follow. This route is not popular and you are unlikely to meet other walkers until you emerge onto the Carrauntoohil to Caher Ridge.

Because it is on the north side this route would be too steep on a morning when ice has formed, and the ground is slippery. However, with an ice-axe and crampons the slope could be scaled.

Always take the route to the east of the Coomloughra lakes – the route around the western side is rather steep.

Inside the Black Mare gully follow the river until you are faced with choices of ascents. All three choices lead quite safely to the summit ridge.

The Reeks Walks

Map 12 - *The Reeks Walk from Dunloe to Glencar*

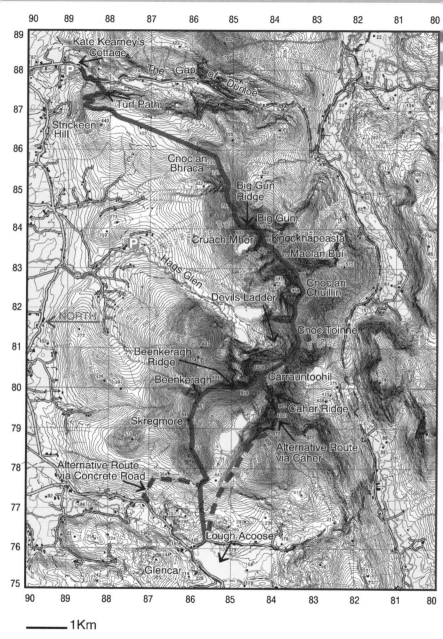

Previous page: *From Cruach Mhór to the Big Gun*

Walk 14

THE GAP OF DUNLOE TO GLENCAR

Summary: This is a long arduous trek from Kate Kearney's Cottage over all the peaks of the Reeks to Beenkeragh and down into Glencar. The walk includes six points that are above 3000 ft.

Until not so long ago this walk was an organised outing for the June Bank Holiday. Sadly this has not survived.

The walk requires the organisation of transport between Glencar and the Gap of Dunloe.

Time: 7 to 9 hours   **Distance:** 18 km   **Ascent:** 1850m

Start and Finish: The traditional route is from Kate Kearney's to Glencar. However, it is acceptable to undertake the route in the opposite direction. Crossing the Big Gun Ridge is generally safer going west.

Escape Routes: The first escape before attempting the Big Gun Ridge is Derrycarna. The next escape would be off Maolán Buí down the Bone into the Hag's Glen. The Zig-zags or the Devil's Ladder offer alternatives to climbing Carrauntoohil. If the Beenkeragh Ridge is to be avoided then a retreat to the Heavenly Gate route or a circuit to O'Shea's Gully are the choices other than Caher.

Route Description   see **map 12** page 116

Park at Kate Kearney's Cottage and walk south into the Gap of Dunloe. After half a kilometre, at **100:87720:88300**, take the path to your right that ascends towards Strickeen Hill. There is a Kerry Mountain Rescue sign fixed to the rock beside the start of the path.

This was the old turf road, where turf cut on the plateau under Strickeen was brought down by donkeys into the valley. The path zig-zags to turn under Strickeen and south into the bog. You will see the remnants of bog excavations and even loose turf strewn in the areas where the bog was worked.

Avoiding Strickeen Hill head south to the first peak which is Cnoc an Bhráca at 731m. You must drop briefly to the col at Eisc an Bhráca before starting the trek up. You will be happy to know that you will not drop below this elevation again until you are descending into Glencar. From Eisc an Bhráca your direction is west-southwest up to Cruach Mhór. There is a large stone grotto built on Cruach Mhór. This is relatively recent in origin. Built by local man, Tommy Sullivan, as an act of worship, it is reputed that he hauled all of the materials up that mountain on a daily basis for over two years. He would sometimes start his task after a hard day's work, moving gravel or water only a few metres before darkness fell. During the summer he would often spend the night on the mountain.

The Big Gun Ridge is directly south of Cruach Mhór and it is a narrow arête that should not be attempted by those who do not have the head for it. It is a series of large boulders that form slabs and peaks. Under the ridge on the western side, and beginning near Cruach Mhór, there is a narrow path. This path takes the walker past the Big Gun and on to Knocknapeasta.

The Big Gun is an exposed peak with ridges before and after it. From here leave the ridge to drop to the south onto a band of rock. This rock band takes you to a gully which leads back onto the ridge.

Knocknapeasta at 988m is the highest peak on the eastern side of the Reeks. If the sun is favourable you may be able to see the wing of a plane in the corrie lake below. (See Walk 5 Cummeenapeasta Circuit)

At Knocknapeasta the ridge widens and the trail is relatively flat over Maolán Buí 973m, Cnoc an Chuillin 958m and Cnoc Toinne. In this area of the Reeks you are more likely to see birds of prey than on any other part. The little meadow pippets, rabbits and hares that frequent these mossy slopes are hunted by falcons and kestrels.

From Cnoc Toinne you now swing to the northwest to drop down to the top of the Devil's Ladder, where you begin the long trudge up to the cross on Carrauntoohil. On Carrauntoohil a decision must be made on whether to go to Beenkeragh or Caher. The descent via Caher will take 2½ hours, whereas via Beenkeragh you must add another ¾ of an hour. The latter is also a more challenging scramble and consequently more dangerous.

At the summit of Carrauntoohil flat rocks prevent route definition. The most defined route, away from the cross and to the south, is the one you have come up from the Devil's Ladder. If you should accidentally walk down away from the cross on the north side, you will find a warning sign with a skull and bones advising you that there is no safe descent here. Beenkeragh is due north but you must first descend to the west-northwest to pick up the path. The route to Caher, conversely, is off to the southwest.

Map 11 and the route description of the Coomloughra Horseshoe should be referenced for whichever choice of descent you have taken.

Walk Times: From Kate Kearney's to the top of the Devil's Ladder will take 4½ to 5 hours. Another ¾ to one hour is required to the summit of Carrauntoohil. Depending on the descent route chosen you then have a minimum of 2½ hours, with a possible 3½ hours via Beenkeragh.

Survival Tips: This trek will take all of a long day, so to attempt it outside of the summer months is not to be recommended. A careful eye needs to be kept on the time to ensure that the walk will be completed during daylight.

At the Big Gun Ridge the very precipitous ridge can be somewhat avoided by dropping to a narrow path on the western side.

After the summit of Carrauntoohil you need to find the route to the Beenkeragh Ridge. This is not easy to find in misty conditions. If you find that you are lost you can head over Caher in a direction northeast. This path will also take you to Glencar.

The Reeks in winter

The Comloughra Horseshoe

Walk 15

THE HAG'S GLEN CIRCUIT

Summary: The Hag's Glen or Coomcallee circuit allows the walker to pack into a day all the beauty that is the Reeks, yet has the advantages of not requiring transport to be arranged and avoids the bog from Strickeen over to Cnoc an Bhráca.

Time: 6½ to 7½ hours   **Distance:** 16 km   **Ascent:** 1500m

Start and Finish: Cronin's Yard or Lisleibane. The walk is outlined walking clockwise.

Escape Routes: Only escape routes down into Hag's Glen are listed here. The first escape can be made directly off Knocknapeasta, the second off the Bone. Further along there is the Zig-zags, then the Devil's Ladder and Heavenly Gates. Beyond Carrauntoohil O'Sheas' Gully offers an escape en route to Beenkeragh.

Route Description   see **map 13** opposite

The route is to enter Hag's Glen and climb directly up to Cruach Mhór. Beginning the climb to the east of Cruach Mhór is an option but it is suggested that the base of the gully known as Eisc an Bhráca is inhospitable. Robust fences west of Cronin's Yard forces the walker to pass the wooded area before turning up towards Cruach Mhór.

From Cruach Mhór over the Big Gun to Knocknapeasta is a series of narrow ridges. If the weather is poor or there are icy conditions, you may want to consider an ascent from the Hag's Glen directly to Knocknapeasta.

Pick up from the previous walk the directions from Cruach Mhór around to Beenkeragh.

From Beenkeragh the descent is northeast towards Knockbrinnea, via *aircraft rock*, then down over the heather to Lisleibane, or dropping off earlier for Cronin's Yard. Avoid the ridge that descends off Knockbrinnea to the east. There is a double summit on Knockbrinnea. The line from the higher one, at 854, east to the slightly lower one at 847 leads on to the precipitous area of the Hag's teeth. From 854 the correct route is northeast.

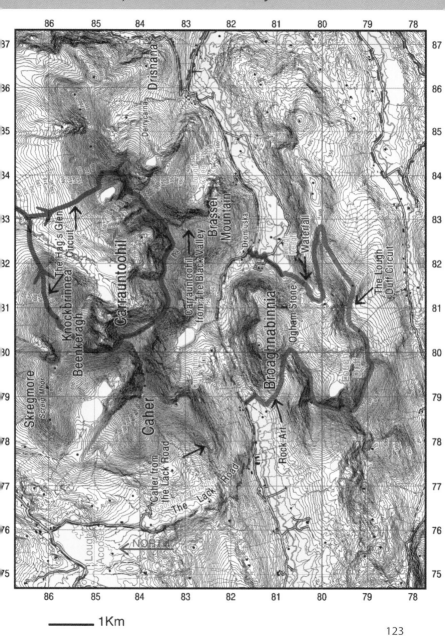

Drishana

Derrycarna

Brassel Mountain

Dromluska

The Hag's Glen Circuit

Carrauntoohil

Knockbrinnea

Beenkeragh

Caher

Skregmore
Sceilg Mhór

Waterfall

The Lough Duff Circuit

Ogham Stone

Carrauntoohil from The Black Valley

Broaghnabinnia

Lough Duff

Rock Art

Caher from the Lack Road

The Lack Road

Lough Acoose

NORTH

1Km

123

The Black Valley and
the Bridia Valley

From the Head of the Gap eastwards to the Upper Lake of Killarney and westwards to Broaghnabinnia is the Black Valley. The mountain of Broaghnabinnia blocks the road westwards and acts as a barrier in the valley. The only way through it is via the narrow Kerry Way path. The valley on the west side of Broaghnabinnia is known as the Bridia Valley. Here the paved road leads to Glencar.

Caher in the foreground, Carrauntoohil in the background

Walk 16

CARRAUNTOOHILL FROM THE BLACK VALLEY

Summary: This is a steep climb over grass up to Curraghmore (whose summit is shown on the 1:25,000 map as Graighin), then a gradual climb to Caher and over the ridge to Carrauntoohil, returning over the top of the Devil's Ladder, Cnoc Toinne and Cnoc an Chuillin to descend via Brassel Mountain. It is a tough trek that will be slippery in wet conditions.

Time: 5 to 6 hours   **Distance:** 11 km   **Ascent:** 1150m

Start and Finish: Under Brassel Mountain at Dromluska.

Escape Routes: Off Curraghmore the safest descent is west to the Lack Road. A careful descent is also available to Curraghmore lake. There is the obvious route down off Carrauntoohil via the Devil's Ladder but this is on the wrong side of the mountain.

Route Description   see **map 13** page **123**

It is possible to drive deep into the Black Valley, taking the road south of Lough Cummeenduff and rejoining the Kerry Way at Dromluska. Within half a kilometre of rejoining the Kerry Way, at **152:82125:81925,** there is a place to park near a sheep enclosure. The alternative is a walk through the Black Valley along the Kerry Way.

From the parking place walk west to the end of the paved road where there is a farmyard. Just beyond the farmyard follow the stream up the mountain to the north that discharges out of Lough Curraghmore. Follow this stream to the lake and circle the lake on the western shore. Into the northwest corner of the lake flows a stream that comes down from the west and Curraghmore. The stream divides as you climb and your route should be to stay with the stream on the left. This is a gentler slope that brings you via a gully to the top of Curraghmore, known as Graighin, at 822m.

From Curraghmore to the Caher summit is a turn to the right and a direction north, then the trail heads off over the Caher humpback to the right and east to drop over a long col under Carrauntoohil.

To return via the route up is quite steep and slippery over the grassy

Brassel Mountain

slopes around Lough Curraghmore. The recommended return is to climb Cnoc Toinne from the Devil's Ladder and to proceed over Cnoc an Chuillin. This is an important point on the route and it is essential to be sure of the position. Check it at **958:82338:83340**.

The Reeks ridge continues to the northeast but your descent is to the southeast. Lough Calee (shown on the 1:25,000 map as *Loch Cuilleann*) is the initial direction but only briefly. After less than half a kilometre you deviate to the south and pick up a stream that swings to the west as it approaches Brassel Mountain. The stream, known as Clashknockbrassel, will take you down to the parking place.

You should notice the shape of the summit of Brassel Mountain, where, during the Ice Age, the flowing ice has rounded the south side, contrasting with the sharp features on the north side. This is the classical feature of a *roche moutonnes*.

Walk Times: From the parking place at Dromluska to the summit of Caher will take up to 3 hours. It is ¾ of an hour to one hour to the summit of Carrauntoohil. The descent is then 1½ to two hours.

Survival Tips: There are steep, dangerous cliffs around Lough Curraghmore, where accidents have occurred. Care is required, especially on the descent, to avoid these steep inclines. Coming down from Cnoc an Chuillin the gradual turn to the south, then to the southwest is important, otherwise you may end up looking down the steep slope to Lough Calee (Loch Cuilleann)

The Lack Road from the Bridia Valley

Walk 17

CAHER FROM THE LACK ROAD

Summary: A very safe and interesting route to Caher, thence if there is the inclination, to Carrauntoohil. There are two choices of starting points – from Lough Acoose or from the Bridia Valley. The ascent is over a relatively gentle gradient, with virtually no scrambling.

Time: 4½ to 5½ hours   **Distance:** 8 km   **Ascent:** 950m

Start and Finish: Either at Derrynafeana, south of Lough Acoose, or at Maghanlawaun in the Bridia Valley. This walk is a route up to Caher, returning the same way.

Route Description   see **map 13** page **123**

For the Derrynafeana start drive in the road around Lough Acoose, going through a gate, then on to where the paved road ends at a crossroads, at **170:76100:84000**. There is parking here for four or five cars. Ensure that you do not block either road and that you have closed the gate. Be aware that this is a private road and that you may not park if the landowner requires you to leave. The Lack Road is a continuation of the road to the right, passing a long derelict building.

In the Bridia Valley there is space for two or three cars where the Kerry Way deviates off the paved road. It is clearly signposted but can be located at **100:77977:81495**. To park it is necessary to drive to the end of the Bridia Valley, through a gate to turn, closing the gate on the way back, and parking tight on the right-hand side near the waymarked sign.

The Lack Road takes its name from the Irish *leac*, meaning slab. It was a purpose-built road that has many flat stone slabs, some quite large. Unfortunately the road is now quite overgrown in places. Its main purpose in the past was to transport butter from Glencar to Killarney. Some have wondered why a road was built over the mountain when there was a perfectly flat alternative road around it to the west.

From either direction the path is marked with marker posts at regular intervals. From the Bridia Valley the initial route is not easy to follow, deviates off the Lack Road, and is partly over a field. The marker posts, however, should assist in following the trail.

At the col the route is east northeast towards Curraghmore. There is a dreadful bog to negotiate first. Once you have passed over this there are vague paths but any route directly up will lead to the same place. One of the paths follows a fence. The trail could not be simpler, with little dangers.

As you approach Curraghmore, if the day is clear, there will be a particularly good view of the Reeks. Curraghmore is shown on the 1:25,000 map as Graighin. From Curraghmore there is a path up to Caher, at 1001m, and another beyond over the humpback towards Carrauntoohil.

Walk Times: From either car park point to the col is half an hour, or a little more from the Bridia Valley. It is then 1½ hours to Curraghmore and a further ¾ hour to the summit of Caher. The return journey will take 1½ hours. If you decide to press on to the summit of Carrauntoohil allow a further two to 2½ hours.

Survival Tips: From the col on the Lack Road to the base of Curraghmore it is necessary to cross a bog, where there are deep, wet areas. Waterproof boots are essential. From either direction it is possible to bypass the bog by veering in the direction of Curraghmore, thus avoiding the col.

At the base of the Bridia Valley route the Kerry Way deviates from the Lack Road to avoid properties near the road. Unfortunately the route is therefore not so easy to follow, so watch out for the marker posts.

There are better parking possibilities in Derrynafeana than in the Bridia Valley. Derrynafeana is higher than Maghanlawaun by 70m.

The isolated rock under Broaghnabinnia which has rock art cut into it

Walk 18

THE LOUGH DUFF CIRCUIT

Summary: The Lough Duff circuit is as fine a ridge walk as any in Ireland. There are many choices of start and finish. The particular route described here avoids the steep summit of Broaghnabinnia. Starting in the secluded and picturesque Bridia Valley, it features the inspection of a feature considered to be ancient stone art.

There is a steep ascent to the Lough Duff ridge and an exhilarating walk along the ridge before descending into the Black Valley, where we return over the Kerry Way to the starting point.

Time: 5 to 6 hours   **Distance:** 15 km   **Ascent:** 780m

There is an alternative walk that circuits Broaghnabinnia, avoids the Lough Duff Ridge and takes in a spectacular waterfall, which reduces the walk to 4 hours.

Start and Finish: At the end of the Bridia Valley, under the mountain of Broaghnabinnia.

Route Description   see **map 13** page 123

Drive into the Bridia Valley around by Glencar and drive to the end of the road where there is a gate. There are very few areas to park. However, if the landowner is nearby enquire if you can park inside his gate where parking is available. At **115:78873:81750** take the dirt track road over the ford in the river. As the dirt track road turns to the left you take a track to the right. This track goes from **105:79135:81481** to **90:78866:81270**, a distance of 200 m, where you will turn due south-southeast.

The stone art is on an isolated rock. Although the Ordnance map indicates it at **143:79020:81036**, it has been positioned by GPS slightly to the west at **149:78910:81070**. The suggestion is that you set your GPS for **79000:81050**. The rock is not that difficult to find once you are in the general vicinity. You may now muse as to whether the fish impression on the rock (on its north face) was cut by metal or stone, or whether it is possibly a fossilised impression left in the rock. The latter would have required the fish to die and be buried in a significant depth of sand in an

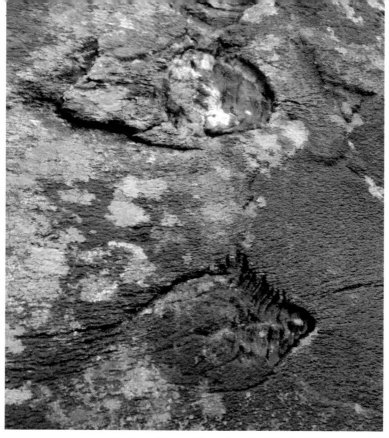

The lower figure of the rock art is a fish, the higher one a shell

upright position – the bedding planes are at right angles to the rack face.

From the stone art the route to the col should be clear up to the east-southeast. The trail is over a wide gully, shown on the map as Coumreagh. The col, known as Bearna Seilge, is boggy and wet. From the col the route is now up to the southwest to gain the narrow rocky ridge, where the ridge then turns to the west on to **665:78888:80248**, before it swings to the south to points 776 and 784 as indicated on the Ordnance maps.

Lough Duff, or *Dúloch*, as it is shown on the 1:25,000 map, translates from the Irish as *black lake*.

From 784 the route is east-southeast. There is now a steep descent. You should head for **700:79710:78900** before dropping down to the west to a col. Point 568 is to the northeast, from where you will descend to another col to the east and on to the western summit of Knocknabreeda at **569:81505:79343**. We now have to find a safe descent off the eastern side of Knocknabreeda. This is best achieved by heading east-northeast to the next col, then contouring back to the west to descend into the Gearhameen River valley.

Cross the river and then follow it around to the spectacular waterfall above Lough Reagh. There is an Ogham stone, not shown on the Ordnance map, on the western side of Lough Reagh, roughly at 81600:80800. On the northwest shore of Lough Reagh there is a dirt-track road that leads out to the paved road in Cummeenduff. Turn left and follow the Kerry Way back into the Bridia Valley. En route the waymarked trail passes an obelisk and diverges through rocky fields to avoid a farmhouse.

Survival Tips: The walk over the ridge is not suitable when the weather is wet. There are some parts that are over rocks, on narrow ridges, where it will be slippery. Similarly the walk is not suitable along the ridge in windy conditions.

Bearna Seilge, the col between Broaghnabinnia and the Lough Duff ridge, is very wet and boggy.

The Gearhameen River falls into Lough Reagh

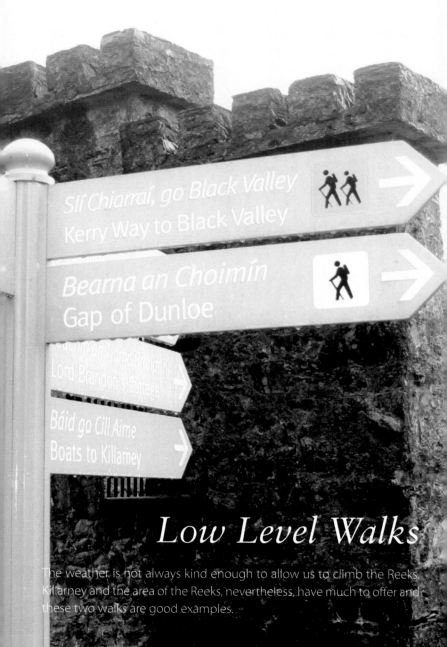

Slí Chiarraí, go Black Valley
Kerry Way to Black Valley

Bearna an Choimín
Gap of Dunloe

Sráchín an Tiarna Brandon
Lord Brandon's Cottage

Báid go Cill Airne
Boats to Killarney

Low Level Walks

The weather is not always kind enough to allow us to climb the Reeks.
Killarney and the area of the Reeks, nevertheless, have much to offer and
these two walks are good examples.

Walk 19

THE GAP OF DUNLOE TO DERRYCUNNIHY CHURCH

Summary: This walk is over roads from Kate Kearney's Cottage through the Gap of Dunloe, into the Black Valley, eastwards into the Killarney National Park. The choices are then to either take a boat trip over to Killarney, returning to Kate Kearney's by bus, or to walk to a prearranged transport point on the road from Kenmare to Killarney. Of course, there is always the further alternative of retracing one's steps back to Kate Kearney's.

Walk Times: It is 2 to 2½ hours from Kate Kearney's to Lord Brandon's Cottage and another 1½ to 2 hours to Derrycunnihy Church.

Time: 5 hours   **Distance:** 16 km   **Ascent:** 180m

Start and Finish: Start at Kate Kearney's Cottage. Finish at Derrycunnihy Church.

Escape Routes: The route is very popular during the summer, where tourists take a jaunting car ride, instead of walking, to the National Park. If the legs are not prepared for a 13 km walk, then perhaps the jaunting car option is to be considered.

Route Description   see **map 14** page 137

Park opposite Kate Kearney's Cottage and walk south into the Gap of Dunloe (see Walk 1). Through the Head of the Gap the road drops to a road junction, where you turn left into the Black Valley.

From here you will follow the signs for Lord Brandon's Cottage. Passing the Black Valley Church on your right you will come to another road junction, where you will take the road to the left. Within 50m there is another junction. Bear right. The road now follows the Gearhameen River, which flows into the Upper Lake of Killarney.

The roads are surfaced in tarmac down into the Black Valley and are dirt track along the Gearhameen River. From the entry to the Black Valley to Derrycunnihy Church the route follows the Kerry Way.

In the Black Valley the rock outcropping on the valley floor has been smoothed and rounded during the ice age, and you will note the grooves cut into it by boulders embedded in the ice, as the ice dragged them over the underlying rocks. These grooves are known as *glacial striae*.

Beside the Black Valley church is the Youth Hostel, run by the Tangney family who have lived in the Black Valley for several centuries. There is a small shop beside the hostel.

Lord Brandon's Cottage is over a pedestrian stone bridge, clearly signposted. The building is now a fine, spacious restaurant, with toilet facilities at the side. The bridge was once a toll bridge. Butter from Glencar was brought over the Lack Road, through the Black Valley and into Killarney, before being sent on its way to Cork.

You may now walk from the Cottage, around the lake into Killarney, but this adds 16 km to the 14 km already covered. The alternative is to take a boat trip over to Ross Castle. Near Ross Castle there is an old copper mine that dates to the early part of the nineteenth century.

It may be more practical for a full day's walk to continue on foot around the Upper Lake of Killarney, on its southern shore, through the Derrycunnihy Oak Woods and out onto the N71 main road from Kenmare to Killarney. There is a disused church on the road, near Galway's Bridge, that has a lay-by where parking is available. This is Derrycunnihy Church.

Survival Tips: Walking boots are recommended, though not essential for this walk. The route is over tarmac or dirt track roads where walking shoes may be more comfortable. The stiffest part of the journey is the climb up to the head of the Gap. In the National Park, after a 13 km walk, there is an excellent refuge at Lord Brandon's Cottage. This is a restaurant (only open in the summer) that has toilet facilities. So, it may not be essential to carry food and drink. Lake flooding may make this route impassable.

Black Valley Church

Map 14 - The Gap of Dunloe to Derrycunnihy

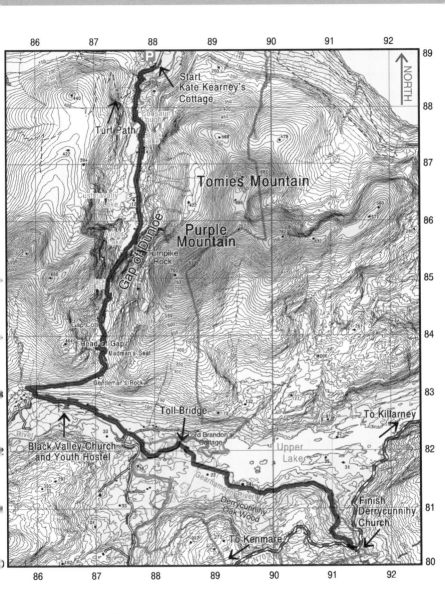

1Km

Near the head of the Gap of Dunloe

Walk 20

THE KERRY WAY THROUGH THE BLACK VALLEY TO LOUGH ACOOSE

The Kerry Way is a circuitous walking route around the Iveragh Peninsula. It is over 100 km in length, going from Killarney through the National Park, to circle the Reeks to the south, over to Lough Acoose and Glencar, north to Glenbeigh, then west towards Caherciveen, south to Sneem and back to Killarney.

In the area of the Reeks the Kerry Way goes through the Black Valley and climbs over a pass, known as the Lack Road, to drop into the picturesque valley of Derrynafeana, which has Lough Acoose at its head. Transport arrangements must be made before starting this walk. From Cummeenduff, under Brassel Mountain, to Lough Acoose is a walk of 15 km, and there is no vehicular road to reduce this length. From Lúib an Bhóthair to Cummeenduff is a further 7 km (or 9 km to the Head of the Gap), but this can be by car. The choices therefore are either a 15 km or a 22 km walk (or 24 km from the Head of the Gap).

Summary: This is a walk substantially over paved roads but also over rough countryside. It is a long walk and includes two ascents, one of which is a rise of over 300m towards the end of the journey.

Time: 6 hours **Distance:** 18 km **Ascent:** 530m

Start: The Head of the Gap, or at Lúib an Bhóthair below it in the Black Valley.

Finish: Lough Acoose, or at Derrynafeana.

Route Description   see **map 13** page **123**

From the Head of the Gap it is a leisurely walk west into the Black Valley towards Brassel Mountain. At **84:84970:82212** you will reach a road junction. The Kerry Way continues straight ahead; the road to the left goes around the Cummeenduff Lakes and you will meet it again at Dromluska. A farmyard defines the end of the paved road and the beginning of a dirt track road, then it is on under Brassel Mountain to meet the paved road again at Dromluska.

Follow the road towards the obvious col that separates Broaghnabinnia from the lower slopes of the Reeks, passing a large obelisk on your right, up to another farmyard. Here the waymarked path deviates to the right to avoid the farm, through stony fields. Cross a wooden bridge and then climb to the col.

Through the Black Valley, and down through into the Bridia Valley, the landscape has been shaped during the ice ages. The rock outcropping on the valley floors has been rounded and the surface scraped by boulders being dragged over them by the ice.

As you ascend down from the col watch out for the way markers – the tendency may be to wander too far to the south. As you drop into the Bridia Valley you may form the wrong impression that the route is via the disused farmyard, whereas it is north of this. You will meet the paved road of the Bridia Valley and, after a kilometre, just beside a house on the left, the Kerry Way deviates off the road to the right. The trail is clearly signposted.

There is now some varied terrain as the Kerry Way is routed around properties and disused farm buildings. You join the old Lack Road high on the slope. The term lack road comes from the Irish word *leac*, meaning slab of rock. It is not hard to see why the road has this name. Flat stone slabs, some of quite enormous size, were gathered and laid along the outer edge of the road. The Lack Road, or *Bóthar na Lice*, is an ancient road once used mainly for the transportation of butter from Glencar to Killarney. It zig-zags up to a col from where there are fine views of the Reeks and the valley down to Lough Acoose.

It is a leisurely 2 km down to the townland of Derrynafeana, an area obviously much more populated in the past, where you will pick up the paved road out to Lough Acoose.

Survival Tips: The name Lack Road may give the impression that the route is paved underfoot. Not so – the Lack Road is quite overgrown; the Kerry Way has been routed around properties in the Bridia Valley, over fields. Consequently the route is rough and in winter will require good walking boots.

There are some parking spaces at Derrynafeana, south of Lough Acoose that can shorten the journey.

REFERENCES AND FURTHER READING

Foclóir Gaeilge – Béarla, Irish-English Dictionary, published by the Department of Education.

Toponomia Hiberniae Barony of Dunkerron North, by Breandán Ó Cíobháin, published by Dún Ciaráin Thuaidh.

The Geology of Ireland by J.K. Charlesworth, published by Oliver and Boyd.

Geology of Kerry-Cork by M. Pracht of the Geological Survey of Ireland, 1997.

The Irish Landscape by Charles Hepworth, published by Dunedin Academic Press.

Kerry, A Natural History, by Terry Carruthers, published by The Collins Press.

Flora Hibernica by Jonathan Pilcher and Valerie Hall, published by The Collins Press.

Complete Irish Wildlife by Derek Mooney, published by Harper Collins.

Killarney National Park edited by Bill Quirke, published by The Collins Press.

The Iveragh Peninsula, 50 walks and scrambles around Killarney, by Barry Keane, published by The Collins Press.

Notes